This book was donated
thanks to many
generous contributions
made to:

The Library Tribute Fund

1999

TRIBUTE
FUND

PROPAGANDA & DREAMS

PHOTOGRAPHING THE 1930S IN THE USSR AND THE US

LEAH BENDAVID-VAL

Edition **Stemmle**

ZURICH   NEW YORK

Consulting and logistical support for *Propaganda & Dreams* in Russia was provided by

Nikolai Romanov   Felix Rosenthal
Yuri Rybchinski   Yevgeny Berrezner
Alexander Lapin   Olga F. Romanova

The following institutions generously encouraged, supported, and participated in the project

The Corcoran Gallery of Art, Washington DC
The Library of Congress of the United States
The Ministry of Culture of the Russian Federation

This book is published on the occasion of the exhibition
Propaganda & Dreams: Photographing the 1930s in the USSR and the US,
curated by Leah Bendavid-Val and organized by The Corcoran Gallery of Art, Washington DC,
July 3 to October 3, 1999.

Propaganda & Dreams
is made possible by a generous grant
from Chemonics International Inc.

and by Kodak Professional in Moscow
who supported the project with photographic materials.

©1999 by Leah Bendavid-Val, Washington DC, and
Stemmle Publishers GmbH/Edition Stemmle,
Thalwil/Zurich (Switzerland) and New York

Editorial direction by Walton Rawls
Designed by Alex Castro, Castro/Arts, Baltimore
Printed by Kündig Druck AG, Baar/Zug, Switzerland
Bound by Buchbinderei Burkhardt AG, Mönchaltorf/Zurich, Switzerland

Photo reproduction copyrights by lenders (see p. 223)
Text copyrights by the authors

The picture captions in this book respect the wording of original editors or photographers as much as
practical, but in some cases they have been altered slightly for clarity or to eliminate material not directly
related to the pictures. For consistency the photographs are dated only by year, unless including the month
makes a special point.

Page 1: Unknown Photographer, *USSR In Construction* proof (Stalin, Voroshilov, removed person,
           unidentified person), mid-1930s
Pages 2–3: Russell Lee, *Fat Stock Show, San Angelo, Texas*, 1940

ISBN 3-908161-80-0 Book Edition

CONTENTS

ARKADY SHAIKHET, *Tillage, hamlet of Kolomenskoye*, 1927   DOROTHEA LANGE, *Migrant agricultural worker's family, Nipomo, California*, 1936

PREFACE

In the spring of 1989, while waiting for an appointment at Moscow's Novosti Press Agency, I flipped through an old anthology of Soviet photographs and came upon some compelling pictures of a farm woman working in a field. Fully engaged in her sweaty job of planting, at the same time caring for her infant, she still managed to appear confident and purposeful, somehow enlarged by her gritty work. This was quintessential Socialist Realism, yet I was oddly struck by the similarities of this and other Soviet pictures to American photographs of the same period; in both countries the subjects were people with tough lives we could care about, and the photography mingled realism with romance, albeit in varying ways and degrees.

The American pictures the Russian woman brought to mind, those taken by the 1930s Farm Security Administration, had never coincided in my consciousness with Socialist Realist pictures made almost simultaneously. Now they appeared to have a significant connection to each other. Both were generated by governments for causes that were shared by the photographers who took the pictures, the authorities who funded them, and the publishers who disseminated them. Underlying the photographs in both countries were the firmly held beliefs that hard, consuming work was not demeaning but elevating, that machines meant progress, and that government public works could make people's lives better. But this certainly wasn't to say that in our vastly different cultures the photographic contrasts were not enormous and easily seen—the earthy heroics of one versus the down-home humbleness of the other.

Pictures that aimed to refocus the American dream during the Great Depression and those that were made to advance the Soviet utopian dream have informed all of us and given us national and personal memories. And, in turn, these memories themselves are noteworthy for their shiftiness, and intriguing for their effect on how we see the pictures.

So, early in 1995, I set out to study the Soviet pictures in earnest. With the help of generous Russian friends met on earlier projects, I visited families, archives, and collectors in Moscow, St. Petersburg, and elsewhere, both inside and outside of Russia. The nearly boundless readiness to share photographs and stories gave unexpected emotional meaning to the consistently thought-provoking effort.

To select American images to go with the Soviet pictures, I searched the immense holdings of the Library of Congress, where about 88,000 photographs are filed in easily accessible drawers maintained by the Prints and Photographs Division. In light of the heartbreaking lack of resources available to preserve Soviet photography, the facilities seem like a great gift. The Corcoran Gallery of Art helped obtain the FSA prints I selected at the Library of Congress.

In Russia I was privileged to spend time with several former Soviet photographers who had worked in the 1930s. They, along with the wives, sons, and daughters of other photographers of the period, offered hospitality and warm conversation over and over again. Evgeny Khaldei, sitting on his bed in his modest apartment, let me hold his exquisite glass plates over morning and afternoon glasses of cognac. He died in October 1997 at the age of eighty. Mark Markov-Grinberg, who celebrated his ninetieth birthday on November 27, 1997, told me dozens of stories with a sly, delicious wit and said on several occasions, "I just want to live to see this project completed." I dedicate this book to all the Russians who gave so much, but especially to him.

Leah Bendavid-Val

FOREWORD

PROPAGANDA & DREAMS: PHOTOGRAPHING THE 1930S IN THE USSR AND THE US provides images of a critical historical time in both countries. The USSR was using photography to create utopian hopes that masked massive repression that verged on governmental genocide against large numbers of its own people. The USA was trying to rediscover its better self in the wake of an economic depression by commissioning artists to depict the real face of their country. While many images from one country may appear similar to those in the other, the photographers who made them worked under radically different systems. Yet, in both instances, their own beliefs and talents shaped the way they exercised their photographic assignments. Photography, however, shows only carefully chosen slices of reality, and it can conceal as well as reveal the differences between a totalitarian and a democratic society.

The Library of Congress is a partner with Leah Bendavid-Val and the Corcoran Gallery of Art in this project. The Library's photography curators, Beverly W. Brannan and Verna Posever Curtis, provided research guidance and assistance with planning and programming for the exhibition. The Library of Congress was the primary resource for the Farm Security Administration photographs in the book and exhibition.

The work by staff photographers for the US Department of Agriculture's Farm Security Administration was an experiment to lend visual credence to the impact of America's depressed economy and World War II on ordinary people living on farms and in cities and towns throughout the country. These pictures come from a remarkably reflective series of photographs produced under the direction and with the encouragement of Roy E. Stryker, the devoted manager of the Historical Section of the FSA's Division of Information. They were, from the beginning, made available to the public—at first through a topically organized picture resource file that the FSA produced for newspapers, magazines, writers, and publishers. When the project was terminated and materials were transferred to the Library of Congress, a wider public was given access. This transfer for permanent safekeeping resulted from Stryker's determination to save the photographs and from the foresight of Archibald MacLeish, the distinguished poet who served as a visionary Librarian of Congress from 1939 to 1944.

Since the arrival of the collection in the Library's Prints and Photographs Division in 1946, thousands of researchers have pored through the browsing files and companion materials: handmade photobooks, official written records, and project scrapbooks filled with newspaper and magazine articles that used FSA photographs. An FSA-related book collection assembles most of the books and reports that influenced the project and also that resulted from it. These materials, along with the microfilm of Roy E. Stryker's personal papers and select transcripts of oral interviews in the Prints and Photographs Division of the Library of Congress, provide an incomparable collective portrait of America in this era. Starting in 1998, an electronic catalog of FSA images and records is being made accessible to an ever-broadening audience on the World Wide Web. It will contain all 164,000 negatives in the collection, including those previously unprinted.

The Library continues to supplement this exceedingly rich and famous FSA collection with other photographic work from the same era. Through copyright, the Library has acquired the now rare film productions of the New York-based Film and Photo League. The recent purchase by the Library's James Madison Council of photographer Aaron Siskind's *The Harlem Document* in its most complete form, exemplifies the work of the Photo League, the successor to the Film and Photo League. It is a photographic record of 202 square blocks of the urban life of the more than 250,000 African-American inhabitants of Harlem from 1938 to 1940. The vast motion picture resources in the Library of Congress include the classic Resettlement Administration films, *The Plow That Broke the Plains* and *The River* by Pare Lorentz, depicting the human relationship with the environment.

Film and photographic material form one facet of the rich resources within the Library from the era of the New Deal and early World War II. Others include the Historic American Buildings Survey (which is now online), and the vast archives of the Federal Theater Project, the Ex-Slave Narrative collection, the Folklore and Social-Ethnic Studies collection, the State Guide book series and unpublished Works Progress Administration materials, and a large collection of prints and posters produced under the WPA, as well as the personal papers of many of America's leading figures from the New Deal period.

The Library also has long held vast resources for cross-cultural comparisons—including the largest collection of Russian print and non-print materials outside of Russia. The purchase in 1906 of the 100,000-volume private library assembled by Gennadii Vasil'evich Yudin of Krasnoyarsk, Siberia, was its foundation. Among the most stellar of the Library's visual collections is the photographic work of Sergei Prokudin-Gorskii, acquired in 1948 in the form of 4,500 images. This extraordinary body of material represents the only existing record of much of the architecture and way of life throughout the Russian Empire during the period 1909 to 1912, including many places that have long been destroyed.

In recent years, the Library has collected visual materials from the Soviet era. The photo-derived posters of Gustav Klutsis; Viktor Deni's poster archive; Tass posters from 1941 to 1945; many films, including copies of all of Sergei Eisenstein's major films spanning 1925-1946 from the Russian Gosfilmofond archive; and selected photographs by Alexander Rodchenko, Georgi Zelma, and Yevgeny Khaldei. While photographs were held by the official news agencies in the USSR, larger bodies of prints and archives of negatives often remained with the photographers themselves. To locate and safeguard this work is an important mission.

The Library of Congress has a longstanding commitment to preserve and provide access to great bodies of special materials that provide background for scholars and others. Because of this commitment on behalf of the American people, the Library has been an unparalleled source of reference for this project and for the broader study of the relationship of photography to society.

JAMES H. BILLINGTON
The Librarian of Congress

ALEXANDER RODCHENKO, *Boys in a boat*, 1933

"The facts of our homes and times, shown surgically, without the intrusion of the poet's or painter's comment or necessary distortion, are the unique contemporary field of the photographer. . . . It is the camera that today reveals our disasters and our claims to divinity. . . ."

Lincoln Kirstein, American Art Critic, 1938

BEN SHAHN, *Children of rehabilitation client, Maria Plantation, Arkansas,* 1935

A. UZLYAN, *A day in the life of Kolkhoz member Grigorenko,* 1939

JACK DELANO, *Mrs. Heatherington, wife of FSA tenant purchase client, Townsend (vicinity), New York*, 1940

"I consider as conservative the conviction that you can only convey what you see, and never, ever go beyond that. That is incorrect. I think that only the method of reconstructing an event . . . can demonstrate all our achievements, given our colossal Socialist construction program."

Max Alpert, Soviet Photographer, 1930

DMITRI DEBABOV, *Construction of Magnitka,* 1930

JACK DELANO, *TVA drillers, Fort Loudon Dam, Tennessee*, 1942

ANATOLY SKUIRKHIN, *Distinguished Miner Akim Ivanovich Terekhov, Kuzbass,* 1932

RUSSELL LEE, *Oil field worker, Seminole Oil Field, Oklahoma*, 1939

"... photography ... does not simply reflect reality, but lends it a transfigured aspect ... the photographic lens has never been objective."

Proletarskoye Foto, 1932

Mark Markov-Grinberg, *Traffic policeman on Old Arbat Street, Moscow*, 1936

John Vachon, *Clark Street, Chicago, Illinois*, 1940

Unknown Photographer, *Communal kitchen, Leningrad,* 1937

"I helped get the camera ready and we stood away and I watched what would be trapped, possessed, fertilized, in the leisures and shyness which are a phase of all love for any object: searching out and registering in myself all its lines, planes, stresses of relationship. . . ."

James Agee, American Writer, 1939

WALKER EVANS, *Washroom and kitchen of Floyd Burroughs's cabin, Hale County, Alabama,* 1936

BORIS IGNATOVICH, *Storeys in a building designed by Le Corbusier, Moscow,* 1933

CARL MYDANS, *Identical houses, Manville, New Jersey,* 1936

Arkady Shishkin, *Commune Dawn, Karelia Region,* 1931

"It is high time to get back to fundamentals. It is high time to admit with courage that we are in the midst of an emergency at least equal to that of war. Let us mobilize to meet it."

Franklin Delano Roosevelt, Radio Address April 7, 1932

DOROTHEA LANGE, *Filipinos cutting lettuce, Salinas, California,* 1933

GEORGY PETRUSOV, *Dnyeproges hydroelectric power station*, 1934

UNKNOWN PHOTOGRAPHER, *Boulder Dam between Arizona and Nevada*, 1936

THE LAST TOAST

I drink to our ruined house,
to the dolor of my life,
to our loneliness together;
and to you I raise my glass,

to lying lips that have betrayed us,
to dead-cold, pitiless eyes,
and to the hard realities:
that the world is brutal and coarse
that God in fact has not saved us.

Anna Akhmatova, Russian Poet, 1934

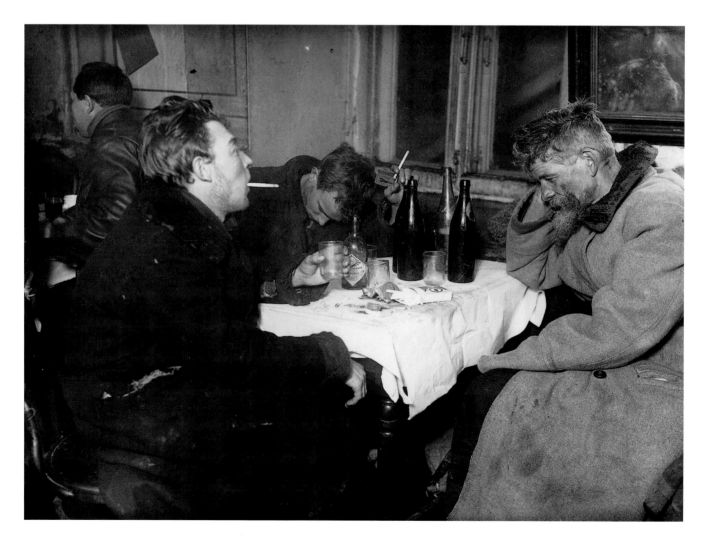

UNKNOWN PHOTOGRAPHER, *Drunkenness, Kharkov,* 1932

Russell Lee, *Saturday night in a saloon, Craigsville, Minnesota,* 1937

"With no cost and no fuss one can make a retouching setup from an icon case. The back of the case is removed, the case is propped up, paper and a piece of glass is inserted. The angle for working can be adjusted, and the interior can be used for pencil, paint, and eraser storage."

Soviet Foto, 1930

NIKOLAI KULESHOV, *Toy factory,* 1931

"The candid-camera is the greatest liar in the photographic family,
shaming the patient hand retoucher as an innocent fibber. . . .
With its great pretensions to accuracy, its promise of sensational truth. . .
[it] presents an inversion of truth, a kind of accidental revelation which
does far more to hide the real fact of what is going on than to explode it."

Lincoln Kirstein, American art critic, 1938

Ben Shahn, *Untitled (Lower East Side), New York City,* 1936

"We are discovering all the miracles of photography as if in some wonderful fantasy, as if in a dream, and they are now becoming an astounding reality. . . . Photography has every right—it merits this—to be regarded with deserving attention and respect as the art of today."

Alexander Rodchenko, Soviet artist, 1934

UNKNOWN PHOTOGRAPHER, *Crimean Resort, Yalta,* 1938

Russell Lee, *Roadhouse, Raceland, Louisiana,* 1938

UNKNOWN PHOTOGRAPHER, *Physical culture team of Pioneers and schoolchildren, Minsk, Belorussia*, 1935

PHOTOGRAPHING THE 1930S
DIFFERENCES IN FOCUS

RUSSELL LEE, *Highway from an automobile, Bexar County, Texas*, 1940

THEY DANCED AND WE DANCED. They built dams and steel mills, planted and harvested, went hungry, nursed their children, and so did we. And in both Russia and the United States we photographed all of that. We believed photography could show if anything was wrong and how things might get better. And it could do this chiefly by revealing the truth. But truth seems less clear to us now than it did to people of the 1930s, and even they differed amongst themselves over it. When the 1930s opened, the citizens of both countries thought that technology would be a panacea, a road to wealth, health, and the better life that all aspired to. But the circumstances and prescriptions for the future in each country couldn't have been more different.

The Soviet people were still reeling from the political and economic cataclysms of more than a dozen years of severe upheaval—World War, Revolution, Civil War, economic dislocations. The Russian Revolution had finally overthrown centuries of despotic rule, and in the emerging Soviet Union a radically new kind of government offered, at least in theory, relief for the long-oppressed masses, a socialism implemented in stages where all citizens would contribute according to their abilities and be provided for according to their needs. The historical antithesis of this "classless" society was found in the wealth-based stratification of US capitalism, where everyone was expected to look out for his own advantage, and society as a whole would be the better for it. The enviable American standard of living had seemed ample testament to this way of life, despite a few hitches, nearly all the way through the Roaring Twenties: great fortunes were being made every day (with other people's money), as "investors" borrowed to the hilt and speculated on yet another potential success in the stock market. But the day of reckoning came, as it had for the Russian monarchy a decade or so earlier.

In both countries the thirties actually started a year early, in 1929: Stalin, who had instituted his first five-year plan the year before, finally consolidated absolute political control over his industrially undeveloped country and the high-flying American stock market catastrophically crashed, setting off a crisis for world capitalism that led to the Great Depression. Whereas the Soviet Union was filled with hope, America's future now looked bleak. The two great countries were at a crossroads, one going up, and the other going down, or so it seemed.

For leaders in both countries huge social and economic problems had to be dealt with quickly through heroic measures, which they felt only strong governments could possibly direct. Both Soviet and American policymakers developed ambitious centralized schemes for improving their people's welfare. And the two governments enlisted teams of photographers to provide evidence in support of their programs. Comparing the pictures of that period in both countries today, we might feel compelled to say that the Soviets photographed progress while the Americans photographed poverty. In the USSR, the pictures were intended to promulgate the belief that socialism was succeeding in turning a backward agricultural country into a modern industrial power. In the US what the pictures conveyed is that, unfortunately, something had gone badly wrong with the American way of life, that there was widespread poverty the country needed to face, and that the government must do something about it. On one hand the pictures were made to instill pride, and on the other they were made to engage sympathy from those who might be able to help alleviate suffering. In each case, the government allocated significant resources to creating a national self-portrait that would endorse political policies and values. The undertaking and its scale were unprecedented in both countries.

Technology had just made broadly available the new, compact 35 millimeter camera and with it the possibility of spontaneous, previously unobtainable pictures. This opened up new documentary possibilities. Photography, it was thought, provided much stronger evidence about the subjects it recorded than the written word. But photography itself wasn't new, and on some level everyone already understood that the camera could change reality: Weathered faces and old buildings could be made beautiful on film. Everyday objects, normally unnoticed and unimportant, could become unforgettable. Fleeting moments, suddenly halted and made manifest, could be memorialized and held high. Heroes and villains could be created where they didn't exist before.

Obviously photographers chose what to put in their frames—objects, portrait settings, scenes, angles, viewpoints, perspectives; the choice of what to show and how to depict it was up to them. They made a picture convincing by arranging the elements or themselves or simply by waiting for a moment that suited them. They could shoot innumerable frames, select which ones they wanted, and discard the rest. All this was known, yet photography was widely embraced as raw and simple truth, mere mechanical data from the source.

Photography wasn't the only sphere in which seemingly contradictory information and beliefs coexisted. Another realm was industrialization: In the eyes of the American public big business and industry were synonymous with economic and social accomplishment, yet for that same public the dislocations and urbanization underpinning this meant slums, a seemingly permanent underclass, and exploitation, and this was viewed as a threat to the small town, the family farm, the little man. In the USSR citizens went hungry and endured slave labor to build Soviet industry, witnessing purges and terror in the name of it, and still they believed they were better off than the rest of the world, that they belonged to the world's most prosperous, free, and

Alexander Rodchenko,
Portrait of Georgy Petrusov, 1935

classless society. These attitudes, bringing into question the very nature of belief, influenced the course of history.

Lenin early established the principle and laid the groundwork for government control over information and entertainment. Although the tsar had been overthrown, the tradition of rule by edict had not. Eventually a clear and rigid formula would determine the communist culture that was generated from above. Offerings would have a uniformity that would finally become popular (and popularity, the leadership learned, was key to getting the communist message across). But throughout the 1920s avant-garde and traditional artists, vulnerable party functionaries, publishers, journalists, and ordinary people's tastes still had vied for a say over what could be legitimately offered as culture, entertainment, and education. Soviet rulers, in their effort to find the most effective approach to their educational goals, continued to accept a multiplicity of styles and organizations, but they insisted upon art, entertainment, and communication that could be understood by the common man.

Diversity of styles in all media persisted even as Stalin, who had been general secretary of the Communist Party since 1922, continued to out-maneuver rivals for supreme power. In 1928 a group of architects, filmmakers, sculptors, graphic designers, and photographers formed an organization they called Oktober. Among its famous members were Sergei Eisenstein the filmmaker, Gustav Klutsis, creator of photomontages, and Alexander Rodchenko, designer and photographer. The Oktoberists felt that the new era required new media and as yet untried

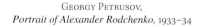

Georgy Petrusov,
Portrait of Alexander Rodchenko, 1933–34

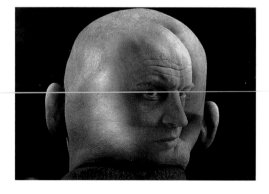

processes, and they wanted to apply mass production to art. Part of their experimenting involved the tearing down of walls between media so that one artist could learn from another. Critic Osip Brik urged this in a 1926 article for the magazine *Sovetskoe Kino* (Soviet Cinema): *Without photographs there is no cinema. Each filmmaker must closely follow the success and progress of photographic art. In it lies the future of cinematography.*[1]

In the late 1920s Soviet magazines had begun to go beyond single images and to feature photographic sequences that described events and told stories. These were repeatedly analyzed politically and artistically. A 1932 magazine piece comparing photo sequences to literature and films acknowledged but did not dwell on the movie camera's capacity to record action through time and space (and omitted dealing with the power a photograph can derive from not showing what is happening outside the frame during, before, and after the picture was taken); the article focused on the principles of organizing the collected material—dealing with the rules of montage:

. . . just like in cinema, [photographic montage] turns a heap of separate shots into a logical sequence . . . there are a large number of tricks used in cinema montage. Tricks used in photo-montage are just as diverse and flexible. A photo artist is limited only by the number of photos and the necessity to develop his story along certain lines.[2]

The resulting ground-breaking picture essays were later emulated by foreign picture magazines.

Some of Oktober's members experimented simultaneously in several media. Others—Elizar Langman,

GEORGY PETRUSOV,
Portrait of Max Alpert, 1934

BORIS IGNATOVICH,
Portrait of Dmitri Debabov, 1930

Dmitri Debabov, and Boris Ignatovich—worked solely in photography, combining journalism with experimental styles. In June 1930 they held an exhibition in Moscow that featured photographs using conventional communist content but unexpected, even startling, angles and crops. Stalin is said to have hated it.

A group that repudiated Oktober's principles, the Union of Russian Proletarian Photographers (ROPF), started its own organization at about the same time. The photojournalists who led it, like Arkady Shaikhet and Max Alpert, stood for straightforward, supposedly unmanipulated reportage. But in fact they too had artistic aspirations.

Photographer Mark Markov-Grinberg, ninety years old when interviewed in 1997, identified with ROPF, but despite that was enchanted by the talent of several Oktoberists. "Rodchenko," he recalled, "could push the picture far toward the diagonal—it worked—and his friend Elizar Langman photographed a plow, a great turn stretching diagonally into the earth—beautiful." But Markov-Grinberg didn't like most of the Oktoberists' work. "Usually their strange angles didn't appeal to us realists; how can you walk on a diagonal horizon? You'd have to be a mountain climber."

Markov-Grinberg was just one of the talented Russian photographers working throughout the 1930s. He started life as Mark Grinberg, born in Rostov on the Don River in 1907. At the end of secondary school he befriended a student both skilled with a camera and in his home darkroom, and, inspired, young Mark took up photography himself. He sold his prized aquarium and fish to buy an old Erneman camera with expandable bellows. "The glass plates I used weren't very sensitive, and I had to hold a shot for hundreds of seconds, even in sunlight," he recalled. His first job in photography was as a stringer for the regional paper *Sovetski Yug* (Soviet South). The paper paid forty kopeks for each photograph, and this was a fortune to him. One day the famous poet Vladimir Mayakovsky came to Rostov. In Russia where poets are revered, this was a big event. "The managing editor said, you'll do the shoot and I'll talk to Mayakovsky," recalls Grinberg. "We knocked on his hotel door, and Mayakovsky opened it in his gray-and-white checked pajamas. I was so nervous I was mumbling instead of talking. Mayakovsky sat near the window, with one side lit and the other dark. How could I get a decent picture? I looked around, took a sheet from his unmade bed, got the editor to hold it to reflect light onto the dark side, and I did the portrait." Before the year was out Grinberg moved to Moscow. His family name was changed from Grinberg to Markov-Grinberg to sound less Jewish. The Mayakovsky portrait still hangs in his dining room.

Alexander Rodchenko, *Pioneer Girl*, 1930 (variants)

Anatoly Skurikhin, *Alexander Rodchenko retouching photographs*, 1934

Markov-Grinberg's opposition to Oktober went beyond aesthetics; like his ROPF colleagues, he thought tilting the camera was wrong in principle. "Chasing the frame dominated content," he says. "We in the opposite group photographed for a reason, a purpose. Art for art's sake is nothing. But still Rodchenko was our teacher and we were friends."

Rodchenko, eight years older than Markov-Grinberg, made his reputation in the 1920s (and even earlier) as a painter, sculptor, graphic artist, and designer, and subsequently as an innovative photographer. His choice of unlikely vantage points, key to his photographic vision, introduced freshness, surprise, and, through that, immediacy. But Rodchenko's

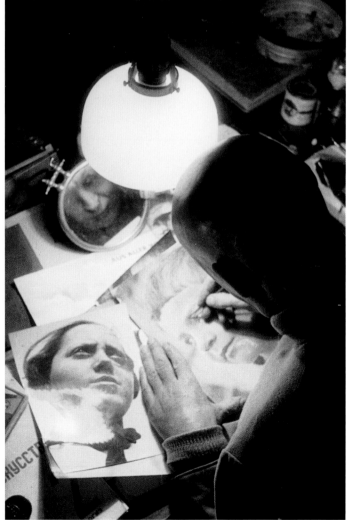

ALEXANDER RODCHENKO, *White Sea Canal*, 1933

YAKOV KHALIP, *New Soviet dirigible*, 1935

unexpected angles were also a statement of authorship (intended or not). As such, his pictures went against the feeling conveyed in documentary-style photographs that the photographer played no role in creating the image other than to be there and trigger the shutter. This, in addition to the unease his pictorial style induced among the authorities, led to repeated official condemnation.

On April 23, 1932, the Communist Party published a "Decree on the Reconstruction of Literary and Artistic Organizations," bringing the period of multiple approaches to a close. The diverse art and literary organizations that had sprung up were abolished. ROPF and its straight photography was the apparent victor and Oktober the ostensible loser in all this, but a glance at the photography suggests nothing so

clear-cut. ROPF members, even those bitterly hostile to Oktober, had begun to use Oktober's unconventional framing, tilts, and diagonals. The remarkable similarity between photojournalist Yakov Khalip's "New Soviet Dirigible," 1935 (above, right), and avant-gardist Rodchenko's "White Sea Canal," 1933 (above, left)—one of myriad examples—is reason enough to avoid the temptation to oversimplify. Deviation from a straight-on, eye-level approach became commonplace, and Rodchenko's trademark was neutralized. And all photographers embraced the approved Soviet themes: industrialization and collectivization, health, science, defense (even in peacetime), and elimination of illiteracy.

A month after the April decree was issued, photographers were further put on notice by an item in the magazine

Proletarskoye Foto (Proletarian Photo) entitled "Public Censure of Photojournalist Langman." To prevent Langman's colleagues from missing the point, this article about his court hearing was introduced with a note: "Here we print the resolution of [the] court, which should be taken into consideration not only by that same Langman."

The court saw the photographs and heard the accusations:

Langman took a formalist approach to the task entrusted to him [shooting a story for the magazine USSR In Construction*], with no consideration for its political significance.*

While at the site [an industrial complex called Krammashstroy], Langman not only failed to contact the social organizations which could have provided guidance for his shoot at the plant, but also ignored the central plan he had been issued.

The shoot done by Langman did not provide a complete depiction of the activities of our socialist industrial complexes; atypical individual aspects of the construction were provided, illustrations of people heroically building the socialist complex were lacking.

These were some of the court's resolutions:

To publicly censure Comrade Langman, informing the Photographic Division of the Press House of this act.

To present to the administration and social organizations a proposal for the political education of Langman and other photojournalists to promote . . . socialist labor in their work.

To present to the administration a proposal for photojournalists to turn in their negatives to publishing house archives for the purpose of thwarting their commercial aspirations.

Now nonconforming artists would be branded "enemies of the people"—lumped together with the old intelligentsia, prosperous kulaks, and the NEP-men who had taken advantage of Lenin's New Economic Policy that relaxed economic constraints for several years.

So within fifteen years, the reshaping of Russian culture that had begun in 1917 was complete. Socialist heroes pre-

YEVGENY KHALDEI, *Pasha Angelina, first woman tractor driver, Ukraine*, 1936

vailed and were the stars of Soviet cinema and novels. They displayed military or economic courage. They were loyal to the regime in the face of danger and death. And they exhorted the audience to emulate their example.

A few outstanding Soviet workers even became photographic superheroes, who were idolized like movie stars. Young photographer Yevgeny Khaldei (later famous for his remarkable World War II coverage) photographed two of them. One, Angelina Praskovya Nikitichna, born in 1912 in the Ukrainian village of Staro-Byeshevo, started as a farmhand, then learned to drive a tractor. She was called Pasha Angelina and conformed nicely to the regime's need to harness women's labor (which unpredictably paid off in wartime when all men went to the front). She taught tractor driving to other women and was elected a deputy to the Supreme Soviet of the USSR. She once was quoted as saying, "To me as well as to the whole of our Soviet people the term 'tractor' means not only 'a traction machine with an internal combustion engine' but something more. The tractor helped us to change the entire life of the countryside. . . ."[3] Pasha Angelina won the Stalin Prize, two orders of the Red Banner of Labor, the Grand Gold Medal at the Agricultural Exhibition of the Soviet Union, and twice was made a Hero of Socialist Labor. Khaldei's photograph (opposite) appeared in newspapers and calendars.

Record-breaking, hero-miner Alexei Stakhanov became another photographic subject for Khaldei. The government had turned Stakhanov into an icon. His name entered the Soviet lexicon to characterize production achievement: A Stakhanovite, a Stakhanov moment, the Stakhanov Movement. The government gave Stakhanov the only automobile in the Ukrainian Donbass region. (It was made in Nizhni-Novgorod, where Ford Motor Company had installed a plant.) Khaldei photographed Stakhanov with his car, but the picture (right) was never published. "The preferred theme for photographs was people actually working," Khaldei explained.

Two economic programs, harshly instituted by the time the 1930s got under way, reflected Communist Party belief that forcing the backward masses to sweat would push them past otherwise inevitable stages of Marxist economic development, enabling them to skip straight to their dreamed-of prosperity: These were the first five-year plan of 1928–1932, which developed industry, and the collectivization of agriculture, which was begun in 1929. In the face of forced labor, hunger, and a pervasive foreboding that accompanied nightly arrests and unpredictable disappearances, the Soviet people nevertheless, for the most part, optimistically believed in their much-touted utopian future.

YEVGENY KHALDEI, *Miner Alexei Stakhanov and his gift car, Stalino (Now Donetsk), Ukraine*, 1936

MEANWHILE IN THE USA the devastating stock market crash of 1929, which stemmed from unregulated financial speculation, wiped out many family fortunes and shook to the core two deep beliefs: that rugged individualism leads to high accomplishment and that laissez-faire capitalism leads to affluence.

Americans hadn't anticipated the crash and were bewildered. They scorned their new president Herbert Hoover, who appeared reluctant to marshal the power of the federal government in aid of those in distress. But they stopped short of fully blaming Hoover, who had only been in office half a year. Americans still believed that people were responsible for their own destiny, and many felt somehow guilty for

being idle, even as a result of widespread unemployment, which was growing from three to twelve million people.

On city streets, as the Depression began it was more felt than seen—less economic activity, less traffic. But when the hardship became visible it startled people. The breadlines remained vivid in the memory of Yip Harburg, a popular songwriter of the day. He described for oral historian Studs Terkel, three decades later, "a big truck with several people on it, and big cauldrons of hot soup, bread. Fellows with burlap on their shoes were lined up all around Columbus Circle, and went for blocks and blocks around the park, waiting."[4] Taken three thousand miles away in San Francisco Dorothea Lange's 1932 photograph "White Angel Breadline" (left) captured in one man's stance the experience of being in a breadline: In the picture the man's hands are clasped, his jaw is set; his arms shelter an empty tin cup, and, alone, he faces away from the crowd. Lange made the photograph the first day she began taking pictures in the street.

Rural victims of the Depression, tenant farmers who had been forced off land their families had worked for generations, had an advocate in writer John Steinbeck. His Pulitzer Prize–winning epic *The Grapes of Wrath* published in 1939, describes with Old Testament poetics the outcome of depleted soil and soulless mechanization:

. . . the dispossessed were drawn west . . . twenty thousand and fifty thousand and a hundred thousand and two hundred thousand. They streamed over the mountains, hungry and restless—restless as ants, scurrying to find work to do—to lift, to push, to pull, to pick, to cut—anything, any burden to bear, for food.[5]

Shantytowns, nicknamed Hoovervilles, sprang up around the country and overflowed with the homeless and unemployed.

But not all Americans were destitute in the 1930s. And even many who did worry about finances, like their Soviet counterparts found respite in entertainment. Every weekday evening people gathered around radios to listen to *Amos 'n'*

Andy, which George Bernard Shaw mentioned as one of the three things he would never forget about the US. (The Rocky Mountains and the Statue of Liberty were the other two.)[6] Radio also featured ventriloquist Edgar Bergen and his dummy Charlie McCarthy, singer Bing Crosby, pianist Duke Ellington, and social commentator Dale Carnegie who told audiences "How to Win Friends and Influence People."

It was also the decade of Little Orphan Annie, Flash Gordon, Tarzan, and Shirley Temple. Moviegoers saw Fred Astaire and Ginger Rogers in *Carefree,* Clark Gable in *Mutiny on the Bounty,* James Cagney in *Public Enemy,* and Jean Harlow in *Dinner at Eight.*

But the spreading grimness of America in those days rendered escapist entertainment hardly adequate or even available for millions. With industrial production so far down, people wanted economic facts and remedies to their problems. Not only did policymakers offer few solutions to the unemployment, they couldn't even give convincing statistics on how bad it actually was. People had come to distrust public officials and newspapers, which they thought filtered everything through their own political and business interests.

America's public figures were less concerned about incorrect political thinking than their Soviet counterparts, but like them they worried about "wrong" moral impulses. In 1934 the country's Roman Catholic bishops created the National League of Decency. Hollywood eschewed the League's taboos: long kisses, double beds, adultery, the words "damn" and "hell," and all nudity, even for babies.

These unprecedented times called for unprecedented ways to communicate. Newly popular devices—radios and cameras—provided a seemingly firsthand means. These beguiling tools dovetailed with people's hardship in an unlikely formula that stimulated and popularized the filmed, written, and photographed documentary: Reality rather than fiction was its key subject, and reports on people's suffering became a significant creative product of the era.

Variations on documentary photography were thriving simultaneously in Europe, in Germany especially, where distress was fostered by the painful enforcement of League of Nations programs of economic reparations to the victors of World War I. Overcoming political and communications obstacles, some cross-fertilization between countries occurred, but by the 1930s Stalin had virtually eliminated the possibility of spontaneous exchange with the Soviet Union. However, some Soviet-published work did reach the US. It must have entered the consciousness of socially aware American photographers, but Americans didn't seriously study pictures by their Soviet counterparts. They weren't interested or they questioned whether Soviet photography was authentic or relevant. On the other hand, innovative Soviet photographers did strongly inspire socialist agitators in central and northern Europe. They had special impact in Germany during Lenin's lax NEP period in the 1920s. The European "worker photographers" movement, spurred on by Soviet aspirations to create a new proletarian photography, established clubs, published, and exhibited. The innovations in camera manufacture were hotly discussed everywhere among photographers, publishers, and, in the case of the USSR, government officials. The small, light Leica camera invented in Germany in 1924, with changeable lenses added in 1930, allowed for so-called candid pictures in low light conditions. The revolutionary photographic results—intimate and spontaneous looking—had drawn worldwide attention in the early 1930s. By 1932 the USSR had developed a Soviet version of the Leica, which was called the FED after Felix Edmundovich Dzerzhinsky, chairman of the Extraordinary Commission, or CHEKA (predecessor to the KGB). The camera used 35 millimeter film in standard cassettes of 36 exposures. Its lens, carrying the brand name Industar 10 retracted when not in use. A Ukrainian commune, also named FED, organized by Dzerzhinsky in 1927 to house homeless children and minor offenders between the ages of twelve and eighteen, produced the cameras. In the nearby city of Kharkov, a research institute developed a total of eighteen models between 1935 and 1977, though the commune itself folded in 1935. Enthusing over home-produced goods, the newspaper *Izvestia* described the FED as "brilliant," reporting that while 1,800 were manufactured in 1934, production had jumped to 15,000 only a year later. Though most Soviet photographers owned and touted the FED during the 1930s, quietly they managed to obtain Leicas, which were much more highly prized. American photographers tended to remain ambivalent about the 35 millimeter camera altogether and held on to their larger-format Speed Graphics while experimenting tentatively with Leicas (which some considered mere toys).

Starting in the 1920s some American artists grew sympathetic to certain ideas of Karl Marx and believed that through their art they could contribute to bettering the lives of workers. Some organized. The economic disasters of the Great Depression, which lasted throughout the 1930s, added size, strength, and credibility to their efforts. One militant group, the Artist's Union, and its publication *Art Front,* existed from 1934 to 1937. Respected painter Stuart Davis was president. He not only cared about disadvantaged workers but believed he was one of them. He thought artists, like other members of the working class, should organize to fight for jobs, decent wages, and insurance. But it never occurred to Davis to let his class-consciousness interfere with his art: Without giving Socialist Realism a second thought he painted his own cubist visions of urban America.

In 1928 photographers and filmmakers intending to elicit social change through the power of their work had gotten together and founded the Film and Photo League. Like their Soviet counterparts they intuitively linked film and photography but scorned Hollywood. League members believed they could change the world through innovative movies inspired by the likes of Soviet filmmaker Sergei Eisenstein, a genius at juxtaposition and sequencing. One League member, Jay Leyda, went to Moscow in the fall of 1933 to study under Eisenstein. He returned to become curator of the Museum of Modern Art's film department and lived for a time in photographer Walker Evans's apartment. Evans got interested in film but never in communism, which he thought naive and oppressive.

In 1936 two photographers, Sid Grossman and Sol Libsohn, seceded from the League to establish the Photo League as a separate organization. Evans's friends urged him to join but he declined. Its group mentality reminded him of what he disliked in communism.

Photo League members set out to photograph the plight of American workers and to disseminate the results. They taught, exhibited, gave lectures and symposiums, and produced a newsletter called *Photo Notes.* They also undertook multiphotographer projects. A three-year program called the *Harlem Document,* led by Aaron Siskind, looked at the vitality and complexity of that single community. In April 1939 the League sponsored an exhibit of US government photographs by Russell Lee, Dorothea Lange, Arthur Rothstein, and Ben Shahn. They also showed the work of photographer Margaret Bourke-White.

Russia had caught the fancy of adventurous *Fortune* photographer Bourke-White in 1930, not for its politics but for its appeal as forbidden territory. Her expertise in dramatizing machinery seemed tailor-made for the rapid industrialization spurred on by the Soviet Five Year Plan. As part of her effort to get a visa for Russia Bourke-White showed her photographs to Sergei Eisenstein, who was visiting New York at the time. He realized immediately that his government would love her heroic pictures. With his endorsement and additional official machinations Bourke-White managed to untangle nearly inextricable bureaucratic strings to win a Soviet government commission to photograph Soviet industry for Soviet magazines. It was the first of several trips that stretched over a decade.

Everything Bourke-White saw in the USSR looked exciting and positive to her—even imperfections were bathed in a glow of optimism. On her first trip she photographed collective farms around Rostov, a tractor factory in Stalingrad, and the world's largest dam at Dnieprostroi. Her approach and style pleased her sponsors: She arranged and lit machines and people for maximum drama and beauty. The results were sharply textured and detailed. When she returned to the US in 1931 *Fortune* printed her pictures and Simon and Schuster published her book *Eyes on Russia*.

Her theatrical pictures made an impact on her accomplished colleagues and on aspiring photographers as well. The texture of the images impressed still-inexperienced Arthur Rothstein, for instance. But Rothstein and others who eventually took up government work did not employ Bourke-White's methods of manipulation, even if they admired the result. There seemed to be no room for that in their particular documentary approach. (Writer Hartley Howe, later praising the work of Rothstein and his government colleagues, wrote, "Unusual angle shots or trick lighting effects are extremely rare. Actuality always wins in any conflict with artistry."[7] The conviction that content—truthful content— was separate from and superior to form was shared by Americans and Soviets.)

Back again in the USSR Bourke-White photographed more agricultural workers as well as industrial laborers at the giant steel complex in Magnitogorsk. Her radiant reports appeared in the *New York Times Magazine*. Their upbeat opinions reached a fairly wide American audience.

Nevertheless communism never really had a chance in America. For a time radical intellectuals as well as artists believed in the scientific and historical necessity of communism and thought evidence of its rightness could be seen in the USSR. While US factories stood still, Stalin's Five Year Plan seemed to produce jobs and prosperity. The tiny American Communist Party optimistically organized rallies that stunningly drew tens of thousands of the unemployed who were briefly ready to try something new. The party, looked at sympathetically by many who didn't actually join, also organized radical Red trade unions that divided the ranks of existing unions and made enemies in labor circles. The United Auto Workers Union (UAW) was one union where ranks were split. In March 1996 the union's newsletter, *The Ford Worker*, recounted that, "In 1930s redbaiting hysteria, fueled by UAW president Homer Martin, all three Reuther brothers were accused, as were some others, of being Communists. Victor Reuther was removed from his organizing assignment in Flint. At the end of September 1937 he was curtly notified that his services were no longer needed."[8] The turmoil erupted even as Ford Motor Company continued to operate a plant in Soviet Nizhni Novgorod.

Still, Americans needed jobs and food on the table and were searching for clear practical ways to get what they wanted. Ever suspicious of abstract rhetoric, Americans believed in what they could see and experience. And in the 1930s facts and results mattered even more than usual.

To make matters worse for themselves the American Communist Party responded more readily to politics in the USSR than to life at home. Early in the decade members got caught up in the expulsion of so-called counter-revolutionary Trotskyites from their ranks. Later, following Moscow again, they endorsed the Hitler-Stalin pact. With that, the party's fate was sealed. As the decade wore on, party sympathizers had gradually joined the political alliance wrought by Democrat Franklin Roosevelt, who had defeated a Republican Herbert Hoover who failed to rescue the downtrodden.

Roosevelt legislated Depression relief in a New Deal for America that called for an uncharacteristic government expansion into everyday life that was made possible by fear and need. Roosevelt's skill in using the media helped the program. His fireside chats had a ring of authenticity, and radio audiences responded to the president's warm, witty style. He had a unique ability to convince his listeners that they and he shared the same qualities of fairness, decency, and common sense. He used this talent to promote the Democratic Party and his own agenda.

American traditions that exalted individualism fell by the wayside more easily than at any other time in US history, and in a famous Hundred Days Congress passed unprecedented laws that, among other things, created jobs, supported crop prices, and insured bank deposits. The legislation created dozens of new government agencies and attracted idealistic people who came to Washington to make a difference.

One controversial agency, the Resettlement Administration (RA), was established by executive order on April 30, 1935. Renamed the Farm Security Administration (FSA) in 1937, its now well-known program moved poor farmers from their depleted fields to land with richer soil, gave them loans, grants, and price supports, and established experimental rural communities and greenbelt towns on urban edges. Newly settled families participated in cooperative ventures that ranged from sharing heavy equipment to child care, all with government support. Columbia University economist Rexford Guy Tugwell, who had left New York to participate in Roosevelt's Brain Trust of brilliant advisors, headed the complex effort.

To combat criticism that he was merely a leftist with irrelevant academic ideas, Tugwell hired his forty-two-year-old Columbia protégé Roy Emerson Stryker to handle this. Stryker's wordy job description as director of the RA's newly named Historical Section was "to direct the activities of investigators, photographers, economists, sociologists, and statisticians engaged in the accumulation and compilation of reports, statistics, photographic material, vital statistics, agricultural surveys, maps and sketches necessary to make accurate descriptions of the various phases of the Resettlement Administration." In other words, public relations.

Stryker's chief credential was his work on Tugwell's book *American Economic Life,* published in 1933. He had collected and selected the photographs, interpreting and captioning them to reinforce the book's enthusiasm for mechanization and progressive economic policies. This sometimes meant overriding the meaning pictures had had for the photographers who took them. The points Stryker was engaged in making for the book obviously seemed more compelling to him than the intentions of photographers.

When Stryker arrived in Washington in July 1935 photographic archives weren't anything new to government agencies. Mathew Brady's Civil War negatives had been acquired in 1871 by paying off the photographer's long-term storage charges and had resided with the Army Signal Corps for well over a half century. The Bureau of Reclamation and the Geological Survey had pictures of the Far West, the Forest Service had timber pictures, the Tennessee Valley Authority had dam photographs. The US Department of Agriculture, the Department of Interior, the Rural Electrification Agency, and the Soil Conservation Service all had visual records of their work. Images of trees, mountains, livestock, and fields were indexed in hundreds of Washington file drawers. When small cameras and faster film became available in the early thirties, career civil service workers, even non-photographers, could generate pictures on demand. Their photographs, occasionally highly accomplished, were made for the purpose of supporting the government's policies.

Stryker began his eight-year Washington career by mining existing archives to illustrate RA news releases. But within a couple of months, motivated by Tugwell's encouragement and his own growing aspirations, Stryker's plans expanded. He joined the ranks of government officials from New Deal agencies like the Civilian Conservation Corps and the Works Progress Administration in generating new pictures. But no other administrator brought to his photographic efforts anything like the consuming passion Stryker brought. His timing, administrative skills, feisty, tyrannical style, and his belief in the mission he was evolving contributed to an outpouring of contentious creativity. He started to see the Historical Section as a repository for history-in-the-making.

Building the insatiable file, whose gaps seemed to grow as the file itself did, became the insistent, driving motivation behind the goal of providing sympathetic images of his New Deal program to news media.

Stryker sought to fill the file with a moving pictorial report on the great human problem facing the US farm population, but more generally to capture a sweeping portrait of rural and small-town America, a nostalgic portrayal of a disappearing way of life. His view of America gave this envisioned portrait its shape. He wanted pictures of farm fields and country stores, people at home and at work, pictures of churches, movie houses, gas stations, courthouses, and even outhouses. He had apprehensions about urbanization and its threat to old values, sympathy for the dispossessed, and belief in the government programs that would help them. He paradoxically embraced the machine while rejecting its impact on traditional agrarianism.

He was good at cutting through red tape but saw himself as much more than a bureaucrat; he envisioned himself as a historian, sociologist, educator, editor, and occasionally father figure and psychoanalyst. He could justify his agenda to produce a portrait of America by a statement in the Resettlement Administration's 1935 annual report (its first) that the Historical Section's mandate in addition to keeping a record of projects was "perpetuating photographically certain aspects of the American scene which may prove incalculably valuable in time to come."

As the summer of 1935 drew to a close, Stryker began hiring photographers. First he brought in his former student Arthur Rothstein from Columbia University. At Columbia Rothstein had helped Stryker and another professor on a pictorial history of American agriculture.

"I commanded a small task force of students," Rothstein recalled. "We assembled lots of photographs which I copied with my Leica, made prints of, and then turned over to Roy. Roy deposited them in a file cabinet for future use. . . ."[9] Like Mark Grinberg's friend in Russia, Rothstein had been an

BEAUMONT NEWHALL, *John Vachon, Arthur Rothstein, Russell Lee, and Roy Stryker reviewing photographs, Washington, DC, 1938*

amateur photographer with his own basement darkroom since high school. At Columbia, in addition to working for Stryker, he photographed for school publications, earned extra money by taking pictures for students' dissertations, and founded the university Camera Club.

Rothstein didn't really have to move South but, he recalled, ". . . There was a feeling of great excitement in Washington in those days, a feeling you were in on something new and exciting. There was a missionary sense of dedication to this project, of making the world a better place to live."[10]

Stryker sent the new hire to the Blue Ridge Mountains in Virginia where people living in the hills and hollows were to be moved out to make space for Shenandoah National Park. Their way of life was about to be destroyed, and the point of the photography was to record it.

Before Rothstein's departure he and Stryker talked long and deeply about what to photograph. "Roy was the one who made me aware that there is a great deal of significance in

UNKNOWN PHOTOGRAPHER (Probably Paul Taylor), *Portrait of Dorothea Lange, California,* 1936

MARJORY COLLINS, *Self-Portrait at public sale, Lititz, Pennsylvania,* 1942

EDWIN LOCKE, *Portrait of Walker Evans, West Virginia,* 1937

UNKNOWN PHOTOGRAPHER, *Portrait of Marion Post Wolcott with Rolleiflex and Speed Graphic, Vermont,* 1939–40

small details," Rothstein said afterward. "He made me aware that it was important, say, to photograph the corner of a cabin showing an old shoe and a bag of flour; or to get a close-up of a man's face; or to show a window stuffed with rags."[11]

This was different from the college photography Rothstein was used to, and he learned on the job working with a borrowed Leica, its smallness still a novelty. He stayed in a mountain cabin for several weeks. "At the beginning, they were very shy about having their pictures taken, but I would carry my camera along and make no attempt to take pictures," Rothstein remembered. "Finally they got to know me and they didn't mind if I photographed them."[12]

Although Rothstein was the first photographer Stryker hired, he wasn't the first one to work for the RA. The previous June, a month before Stryker arrived in Washington, the head of the RA's separate Division of Information, John Franklin Carter, had signed on photographer Walker Evans to work for the agency on a three-month trial basis. Before going out to photograph government housing in West Virginia and the poverty it supposedly alleviated, Evans ordered 50 pounds of expensive camera equipment from the government. In addition to a Leica, he requested a Deardorff eight-by-ten view camera, a tripod, and plate holders.

On the road in nearly deserted coal country, Evans made portraits and photographed the normally unnoticed facts and everyday surroundings of people's lives—ramshackle houses, churches, signs, commercial establishments. Evans's prints arrived in Washington just after Stryker did and their calm clarity struck him. Opinionated as he was, Stryker still sought Evans's thoughts on the making of worthy photographs. Evans's views expanded his own ideas about the power of straight, unadorned pictures.

ARTHUR ROTHSTEIN,
Self-portrait, Washington, DC, 1937

At about that same time Ben Shahn—painter, poster designer, and friend of Evans—looking to produce photographs he could use as sources for his graphics, met Stryker and got his support for a trip to the same parts of the Old South as Evans had visited. Shahn photographed with a Leica, but did not dwell much on technical quality; sometimes he worked with a right-angle viewfinder so subjects wouldn't know he was photographing them. And he also impressed Stryker with his results. His seemingly helter-skelter pictures, often spilling out of the frame, showed sharecroppers, miners, trappers, berry pickers, and urban dwellers. Shahn appreciated his subjects. He saw their oppressive poverty, but also their vitality in spite of conditions. With similar compassion Shahn also photographed better-off citizens. He shared his opinions with Stryker on how to be persuasive through emotive pictures, and he suggested how to file them, an increasingly complex undertaking.

In a few short weeks Stryker had hired six photographers: Arthur Rothstein, Theodor Jung, Paul Carter, Carl Mydans, Dorothea Lange, and Walker Evans, who was now made permanent. They didn't have much in common, but they all believed they could make America better. "We all believed that we were in some small way contributing to alleviating suffering," Marion Post Wolcott said later, "and possibly, hopefully, influencing government programs for change."[13] They shared this attitude with their boss.

Dorothea Lange was one of the greatest American photographers of the 1930s, or of any period for that matter. Born in Hoboken, New Jersey, in 1895, she grew up on New York's Lower East Side and took up photography after high school. Lange had had a hard childhood: Her father deserted when she was twelve, polio left her slightly lame shortly afterward,

DOROTHEA LANGE, *Wife of migrant laborer with three children, Near Childress, Texas*, 1938 (variants)

and money problems exposed her to life's grim side. At age twenty-two she set out with a girlfriend on a trip around the world that ended abruptly when she was robbed in San Francisco. There, a year later, she opened a portrait studio.

Lange started photographing in the street early in the 1930s, propelled by the Depression's blow to her portrait business and by marital problems. An unfocused restlessness played a role too. Her humanity and astute observation surfaced in her first pictures of breadlines and migrant workers. Explaining the symbolism in one of her photographs to an interviewer she once said, "I wanted to take a picture of a man as he stood in this world . . . with his back against the wall, with his livelihood, like the wheelbarrow, overturned."[14] She worked for Stryker from 1935 to 1939 and never surpassed the photographs she made then. She wasn't alone in this—her colleagues in the FSA also did their best work during the Depression.

One of them, Jack Delano didn't get into the FSA until Rothstein left in 1940. Delano grew up in Philadelphia where he took an interest in destitute fellow citizens, struggled financially himself, and joined the local Artists Union and Federal Arts Project to earn money and work for social causes. Moved by the plight of unemployed miners in the anthracite coal region of Pennsylvania he obtained the funding to live with and photograph a mining family for a month. With the resulting pictures he applied to the Farm Security Administration for a job. He had to wait months for an opening, but eventually he got the following telegram:

Arthur Rothstein resigned. Will work for Look *magazine. Position available for you. Salary $2300 a year plus per diem and mileage. Must have car, know how to drive and have license.*[15]

At first road trips with a camera seemed highly romantic to photographers. "I was a provincial New Yorker," recalled Delano's FSA predecessor and inadvertent benefactor Arthur Rothstein. "It was a wonderful opportunity to be able to

DOROTHEA LANGE, *Destitute picker in California; A 32-year-old mother of seven children (Migrant Mother), Nipomo, California,* 1936

DOROTHEA LANGE, *Migrant agricultural worker's family (Migrant Mother near frames), Nipomo, California,* 1936

travel around the country and see what the rest of the United States was like."[16]

Eventually Stryker's agency produced more than 100,000 pictures, of which 88,000 are held by the Library of Congress in Washington. Fourteen photographers were major contributors to the program. Another two dozen or so participated. Stryker's hires tended to come with little picture-taking experience, but he sent them out with instructions to photograph thoroughly, whatever caught their fancy. This invited the unpredictable. In 1936 an overly zealous Arthur Rothstein moved an old bleached cow skull from a grassy spot to a parched one near Fargo, North Dakota, and reporters sounded an alarm, starting a scandal about the truthfulness of social documentation that rocked the agency. In contrast, unnoticed by the journalism community, both Dorothea Lange and Russell Lee photographed from the back an out-of-the-way miners monument in Bisbee, Arizona—in the course of a single month, May 1940. And John Vachon made a pilgrimage to the same Atlanta neighborhood Walker Evans visited in March 1936 to photograph the same bill-

boards. Photographers knew each other's work, respected it, and responded to it.

Stryker bore up under the inconvenient publicity and the apparent duplication of effort because he believed in the value of photographers' raw or thoughtful seeing and considered their photographs "a new material for the loom of the historian."[17] Yet he unabashedly filtered this documentary vision through his personal feelings about America. He gave assignments based on his viewpoint, judged the result, and disposed of incoming film accordingly. Stryker expected historians to embrace the pictures that remained as the sum total of pertinent material. For him the historian's task was clear: "To collect the fugitive items of a period and arrange them."[18]

The most seasoned photographers in the group—Evans and Lange—had the greatest trouble getting along with Stryker. His paternalism was infuriating to them. He never doubted his right to take full possession of the photographs he had assigned; he not only confidently edited incoming film, he went so far as to punch holes in negatives he consid-

ARTHUR ROTHSTEIN, *Over-grazed land, Pennington County, South Dakota*, 1936

ARTHUR ROTHSTEIN, *Dry and parched earth in the Badlands, Pennington County, South Dakota*, 1936

ered substandard. Evans, working with a view camera, usually shot duplicates for himself in the field. But the spontaneous nature of Lange's photography made that impossible for her. Stryker's policy especially frustrated her, and she fought it. Rothstein, however, defended Stryker, even years later. "If in editing the pictures, Roy Stryker did not include some that perhaps today might be considered great masterpieces, I wouldn't know," he said. "Maybe his judgment was right at the time; maybe he overlooked pictures that were good. In any case, somebody had to make decisions, and as leader of the project, Roy did."[19] Publicity administrators in other agencies acted similarly.

In addition to camera equipment Stryker provided photographers with maps, a thousand-page textbook entitled *North America*, by Professor J. Russell Smith, and his now-famous shooting scripts. He prepared shooting scripts to get material he wanted for his files and what he needed for the bureaucracy. Some scripts were highly detailed, others fairly sketchy. In 1936 and 1937 he asked for pictures of foreclosure notices, families packing up to leave their homes, the effects of drought on people. Later, he sent out a highly detailed script asking everyone to take pictures of "Railroads and their Place in the Life of America." It listed details to be photographed in stations, on platforms, in freight houses, and in the trains themselves.

Excerpts from a script sent on August 26, 1939, to Arthur Rothstein instructed him on photographing Iowa corn families:

I suggest that you hunt some of the following things: . . . empty corn cribs (very important). Good pictures of corn uncut in the field (very important). These pictures should give some sense of corn as a lush crop . . . telling of the good life that is built around this good land.

Saturday afternoon pictures in towns (very important). Farmers purchasing, farmers in banks, farmers looking over machinery. Watch for Sunday church. . . . Emphasize the state fair as a farmer's fair. (I am under no illusion about the state fairs. They have become very smart and have a decided urban

Russell Lee, *This monument is cast in cement, sprayed with molten copper and mounted on a block of Colorado granite, Bisbee, Arizona,* May 1940

Dorothea Lange, *Monument dedicated to the copper miners of Arizona, work of a local sculptor, sponsored by the WPA, Bisbee, Arizona,* May 1940

tinge.) The Iowa State Fair is probably one of the outstanding agricultural fairs in the United States. Keep your camera pointed at the rural side of it. . . .[20]

On July 14, 1938, Roy Stryker offered applicant Marion Post (later known by her married name, Marion Post Wolcott), of Philadelphia's *Evening Bulletin,* a job for $2300 a year with $5,00 a day for expenses while in the field (men and women received identical salaries). The job offer continued:

You will receive four-and-a-half cents a mile when you travel in your own car. This is to pay gasoline, oil, and a certain amount of depreciation. We supply you with film, flashbulbs, and some equipment. If you desire a special camera, or cameras, I am afraid you will have to supply it at the present time. We are able to add new equipment from time to time, and perhaps later on we can arrange to get some things that you particularly want for yourself.[21]

On the road there was a two-way stream of letter-writing. Stryker sent his usual detailed shooting scripts and reading lists, and in late 1938 and early 1939 Post reported with zest and detail on her camera work and field experiences (including what she wore and how bystanders noticed). Her letters drew energetic responses from Stryker. In one letter he wrote:

I know this will probably make you mad, but I can tell you . . . that slacks aren't part of your attire when you are in that back-country. You are a woman, and "a woman can't never be a man!"[22]

Indeed that may have angered her. Maybe it entertained her too. In any case, she kept up a chatty correspondence that also covered more professional matters. On February 24, 1939, she wrote:

The two main reasons for my taking extra exposures with the Speed Graphic were because for quite a few days I had no confidence in the lasting effects of the rangefinder repairs and adjustments, & I had a general feeling of insecurity & lack of confidence. It's hard to get over that in the beginning unless you see your negatives or prints immediately. I'm getting used to it now.[23]

John Vachon, who was born in St. Paul, Minnesota, joined the FSA as a file clerk. He studied the pictures he was told to file and succeeded, in 1938, in getting sent to Nebraska to photograph agricultural programs and the city of Omaha. From then on he was a full-fledged photographer. On April 16, 1940, from Dubuque, Iowa, he wrote his wife Penny about his struggles with his camera and insecurity. His self-doubt echoed Marion Post's and other colleagues' more than he knew:

Walked with Leica from about noon to present time. Managed to expose 2 rolls, all inconsequential of course—same old crap. Must make myself stop taking pictures of signs, billboards, arrangements of unimportant buildings, etc. In fact must use Leica less and less. It's too easy.

Always the first day is discouraging. Self-conscious, afraid to take good pix when see them, talk to myself. Two young couples, very young, obviously just married came out of r.r. tracks Justice of Peace office looking like fine photographs. But I could not. Maybe in a week I'll be able to.[24]

Two days later his spirits rose in spite of his problems, and he wrote Penny again:

Have 1,000,000,000,000 things to do. Changing film is difficult problem, no closets, no light proof toilets. Fear I fogged some under the bed clothes this afternoon.

I must write to Stryker.

Today was a good day. I walked miles and climbed awfully steep hills and got terribly tired.[25]

The letters reveal the effects of lonely road travel for weeks or months at a time. Those who traveled with spouses or companions, like Delano, Lange, and Evans, had it much easier. Stryker cared and kept tabs on all of them. During the day he fought to keep his program alive, to get more money for it. In the evenings, at home, he looked at pictures and wrote letters to photographers.

THERE WAS NO ONE LIKE ROY STRYKER in the USSR. There were no shooting scripts or letters. Nothing was ever written down. Soviet political appointees came and went frequently.

VLADISLAV MIKOSHA, *Demolition of the Cathedral of Christ the Savior, Moscow*, 1931 (film still)

Throughout the 1920s the Soviet bureaucracy swelled, and its parts shifted and fused with powerful, focused results. At first, it was a photo agency named Bureau-Cliche that supplied regional presses with pictures. In time this organization joined the Telegraph Agency of the Soviet Union (TASS). During that same period the All Union Society for Cultural Relations with Foreign Countries (VOKS) established the RussFoto agency, to serve its public relations needs abroad.

Then in 1931 the mega-organization SoyuzFoto was born. It encompassed VOKS and TASS and also absorbed the Amalgamation of State Publishing Houses (OGIZ) and the Magazine and Newspaper Amalgamation (ZhurGazOb'yedineniye).

SoyuzFoto organized branches in the Soviet republics and in industrial centers and built up a photographic staff. It had its pick of photographers from a growing number of professionals and also from a thriving amateur movement—virtually

Vladislav Mikosha, *Demolition of the Cathedral of Christ the Savior, Moscow,* 1931 (film still)

every factory had a photo club by the late 1920s. (Amateur camera clubs were a worldwide phenomenon, popular in America as well at the time.) Through the Soviet clubs aspiring photographers were given access to darkrooms, film, and paper, but in turn they were expected to depict socialist development. Members competed in local photo contests, honed their skills, and were occasionally noticed and hired by SoyuzFoto. (Though pictures had to fulfill government needs, a small number of so-called family photographs by unknown photographers survived. These anonymous pictures are valued more highly today than the signed ones.)

For photographers, the camera could be a means to adventure and even escape. Vladislav Mikosha, who had been forced to document, for Stalin's eyes only, the dynamiting of Moscow's Cathedral of Christ the Savior (page 55 and above), returned home badly shaken and forever after sought assignments that would take him far from Moscow. Young Soviets and their American counterparts had the same desire to get on the road and see unfamiliar places. Dmitri Debabov, drawn by friends from the stage and movie-acting to photography, took up exotic, remote subjects because they excited him: Central Asian cultures and risky outward-bound expeditions that explored Siberia's far north. About a dozen world-class photographers, and another two dozen who were nearly as good, fanned out to the far-flung corners of the Soviet empire.

SoyuzFoto was responsible for all Soviet press and PR pictures except the scientific and technical ones, and the monolithic agency even produced photo chemicals and paper. It assigned photography, processed it, then disseminated from 50 to 600 copies of each selected picture to Soviet newspapers and the foreign press. Sometimes several pictures of an event, like an election, were mounted together in layouts and distributed. "Approved composition was refined to such a degree," says Moscow collector and expert Pavel Khoroshilov, "that different photographers, different places, and different subjects, look identical." Photographer Mark Markov-Grinberg, just getting started in those days, doesn't think it was a bad thing. "You couldn't tell my shots apart from my friends'," he says. "It came out of the creative discussions we constantly had."

For a time photography editor and theoretician Lazar Mezhericher managed SoyuzFoto's Foreign Department. He didn't have the real authority or the bluster of Stryker, but while he was in power his thoughts influenced photographers and his preferences determined who photographed what. Mezhericher held strong opinions on the power of photodocumentary to educate the populace politically. He spoke regularly at meetings of the Soviet Film and Photo Workers' Union, and he published dozens of articles for the photography community. As long as the talk remained non-political—and this is important—splitting hairs about photographic methods was not really dangerous in the early 1930s. It meant that photographers and critics could believe earnestly that criticism and debate would lift the aesthetic and social level of photographic output and supported an illusion of (limited, at best) intellectual freedom.

One of Mezhericher's more daring articles urged editors to unfetter artists. Editors must "unbind the hands of creative

workers and expand their opportunities to modify their creative thought," he wrote. He went on to exhort photographers to pursue their own styles:

It is not, of course, the editor's place to tell you how to take pictures in a new style; that only your creative sense, your understanding of life, can tell you, and an editor should not interfere with your search; what can help you in your search is an editor working more 'liberally,' if we may use that word, than he has acted until now.[26]

In another article Mezhericher panned pictures by photographers Elizar Langman and Alexander Rodchenko, calling their exploration of form a repudiation of content.[27]

But in spite of such criticism photographers could photograph fairly freely within limits most of them found comfortable. However, this didn't guarantee publication. Klavdia Nikolaevna Ignatovich, widow of well-known, avant-garde photographer Boris Ignatovich, says her husband is a good example of neglect: Though he was one of those few laying the foundation of Soviet photography he was largely ignored in his lifetime. He wasn't persecuted, wasn't really considered a threat, but his pictures were rarely published because like Rodchenko's they were labeled "formalist."

Rodchenko himself, in addition to being criticized, was increasingly ignored and went unpublished. His last great photographic project recorded forced labor building a canal that connected the White Sea with the Don River. About 200,000 people died during the construction. One of Rodchenko's photographs is a view from above, bisected diagonally, that shows an orchestra rehearsing in the lower right section of the picture and laborers at work in the upper left (page 140). The image may be portraying the musicians and workers as equals or as people on two sides of a great divide—it is plausible that both meanings were intended. Aleksander Lavrentiev, art historian and Rodchenko's grandson (his mother was Rodchenko's daughter), says, "Rodchenko wanted to show that musicians and workers were equal as citizens—and that they were also

Mark Markov-Grinberg, *Coal miner Izotov (near frames),* 1934

Mark Markov-Grinberg, *Nikita Izotov, Distinguished Miner of Donbass,* 1934

equal targets for someone standing above and alert with his rifle."

Lavrentiev goes on to say, "You can find a hidden layer even in the sports parades because you recognize the artificiality; although the athletes are pretending to be happy, you can see that this is not exactly the case." There is no way to determine the real intention of the photographers. "They praised reality, but it always had the second side," Lavrentiev says.

Photographer Markov-Grinberg was as honest as Rodchenko and Ignatovich, his work as heartfelt, but his style left authorities less troubled. Before setting out in 1934 for Donbass, Ukrainian coal country, to photograph the miner Nikita Izotov (above), he got verbal instructions from an editor and an invitation and journalistic guidance from Mezhericher. "Mezhericher said you have to show a progressive man," Markov-Grinberg recalled. "The Izotov story was meant for foreigners, to show that the miners ate well, were well off. Mezhericher corrected my ideas. But that was it. On site it was up to me."

Markov-Grinberg got along easily with Mezhericher and his other bosses. "What did I need scandal for?" he says. He wanted to be a brilliant photographer with something significant to say. When he took on the Izotov story he went to live with the labor collective before beginning the job, "so they wouldn't regard me as an ordinary photographer," he says. He stayed six months.

His immersion wasn't unique. In order to represent labor convincingly, so that viewers would accept pictures of workers as authentic, and positively, so that audiences would want to identify, Soviet authorities felt photographers should learn the tasks to be photographed, become laborers themselves, and blur the line between observer and observed as much as possible.

Markov-Grinberg relished the approach. "The first time I went down into the mine the men put me through their baptism: In the elevator cage they ordered the operator to go 'four bells,' the speed for lowering freight. I dropped like a stone for 640 meters. They watched my terror, but I passed their test and got into their community." In Nikita Izotov,

Markov-Grinberg saw heroism: "He would think before he cut, like a geologist. He would approach a seam, a deposit with a foot and a head, hew from below then bring it down with his jackhammer. He taught younger men how to do it for free."

The photographs had to convey all this. "When Izotov came up from the mine in his helmet covered with anthracite dust he was like a statue," said Markov-Grinberg. "I concentrated on nuances. Had I shifted, something entirely different would have come out, a different expression. I wanted a resolute head, a bit upraised, looking. The slightest movement and it wouldn't have been the same." He couldn't shoot in the mine itself. "It was full of methane, a very gassy mine," he said. "The flash was open, but even a closed flash wouldn't have been permitted."

Markov-Grinberg says he portrayed reality. "Abroad they had been writing that the miners were hungry, that they had nothing to eat," he recalls. "But the mess halls had everything, three-course meals."

And even Rodchenko may have believed in the Soviet agenda, according to Museum of Modern Art curator Peter Galassi. In a recent, outstanding essay on Rodchenko Galassi wrote, "Rodchenko's acceptance of the canal commission may have involved a degree of capitulation to forces he neither endorsed nor understood. But his writings suggest that he believed the wooden propaganda he had been hired to illustrate. He appears to have thought, or to have convinced himself, that like the prisoners at work on the canal, he would be redeemed by his travails."[28]

Lavrentiev and his Russian colleagues do not find the question of belief as perplexing as Americans do. Photographers certainly believed, at least for a time, in the future their pictures could show. Future dining tables would indeed be full. Goals like providing newspapers with items for the cause of creating a classless society seemed infinitely more legitimate and compelling than making a fastidious record. Some criticism was encouraged. A plant director might be singled out for not being thrifty enough, for example. Furthermore, people adjusted their outlook, their consciousness, to current facts. Photography historian Valeri Stignaev of Moscow's Institute for Art Studies recalls the publication in *Ogonyuk* of NKVD chief Nikolai Yezhov's portrait. Yezhov had been awarded the Order of Lenin and the magazine showed him as a hero, second only to Stalin. Three or four months afterward (following the assassination of Leningrad mayor S. M. Kirov in 1934) Yezhov disappeared. No one was surprised. He was declared an enemy of the people. Stignaev says that the people themselves deleted Yezhov's image from their imaginations. The authorities went to a great deal of trouble to eradicate newly declared enemies from existing pictures, recalling photographs from circulation and skillfully applying airbrushes. Agnia Khalip, married to photographer Yakov Khalip, remembers the day in June 1937 when authorities requested that her husband turn in his suddenly tainted pictures. In return, he was given a receipt (page 60) for his photographs of "enemies of the people." "His life was at stake," his widow says now.

While Mezhericher was in power, up until 1937, he tirelessly searched for new, imaginative ways to employ the evermore dramatic photographs being produced. He studied photography-dissemination in Western countries. In 1932 he wrote:

Western bourgeois society has made entertainment out of the photographic postcard, a form of 'cheap art,' a distraction from the class struggle . . . but the photo card can be put into direct, concrete service of the party line.[29]

He also wrote repeatedly about "a branch of photo art called commercial photography," perceiving its immense power to persuade. He compared advertising pictures with non-commercial examples and wrote: "Commercial photography's best works achieve a higher level of photographic art. Western photo art has been infused with certain realistic juices from its contact with applied functions." He analyzed the "sharp resolution" and the "colorful, contrasting, and energetic treatment of tones." He described the light as "active, concentrated, directed, and often even sliding around." And he discussed texture, "achieved via lighting, resolution, and tone." He wasn't the only Soviet official who saw Socialist Realist applications for Western advertising techniques. They understood that viewers would identify with subjects in the ads and thought much more of advertising than of American documentary photographs of the day.

Mezhericher continually revised his outlook, reorienting his point of view to embrace changing ideas and circumstances. When he saw Georgy Petrusov's theatrical photograph "Dinner in the Field" (page 96) he decided that this highly accomplished stand-alone image was a model for photographers. He also wrote an article entitled "Serial Photography

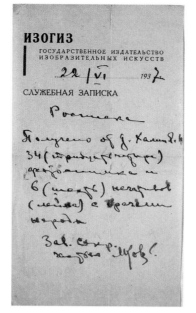

Receipt from State Publishing House for the Pictorial Arts:
"Received from Comrade Khalip Ya. 34 (Thirty Four) Photographs and 6 (Six) Negatives (Leica) Showing Enemies of the People. [SIGNATURE] Director, Security Department, State Publishing House for Pictorial Arts, 22 June 1937"

as the Highest Stage of Photographic Propaganda" and organized for his employers the most influential photography project of its time: "Twenty-Four Hours in the Life of the Filippov Family."

For the Filippov project Mezhericher assigned three photographers to spend four days in July 1931 photographing the carefully chosen Filippov family. Nikolai Filippov, a metal worker in Moscow's Red Proletarian metallurgical plant, lived a modestly prosperous life with his photogenic wife and children. The trio of photographers produced some 80 pictures. Fifty-two of them were made into a picture story. It was praised in Europe and noticed in the US when it was published as a September cover story in the German weekly *Arbeiter Illustrierte Zeitung* (Worker's Illustrated Newspaper).

Ogonyuk reported on the *AIZ* story in October 1931 and *Proletarskoye Foto* analyzed it thoroughly a year later.[31] The *Proletarskoye Foto* article called the photo story a new art form, close to film but with its own requirements, and scrutinized the layout picture by picture. After a lead photograph that "conveys the joy and happiness that fills the whole series," there were panoramic views of Moscow residential areas to set the physical scene and story viewpoint. These establishing pictures include the log house the Filippovs previously lived in and their new modern residence (contrasting not only before with after, but pre-Soviet poverty with Soviet prosperity). The family is introduced at tea, and then its everyday life unfolds hour by hour. The article says:

From this moment on the pace of the story increases. In photos that change rapidly, we see the old Filippov at his lathe, in the plant's canteen . . . his wife at home, in the street taking the little Vitya to the kindergarten, at a cooperative shop. . . . Almost all of these photos are closeups and this is quite understandable. A closeup helps to attract a viewer's attention to a

Soviet Foto No. 2, 1936, praise for western advertising photography: page 16, window glass penetrable by ultraviolet light; page 17, hosiery

Arbeiter Illustrierte Zeitung (German weekly *AIZ*), September 1931 (cover and layouts),
"Twenty-Four Hours in the Life of the Filippov Family"
(Story about a worker in Moscow's Red Proletarian Factory, photographed by Max Alpert, Arkady Shaikhet, and Salomon Tules)

Ogonyok No. 30 (416), 30 October 1931 (report on *AIZ* story about the Filippovs)

standable. *A closeup helps to attract a viewer's attention to a face or to a thing.*

The article further discusses the importance of closeups that "direct our fantasy." The Filippovs' "faces are calm, concentrated and bear a certain 'working class expression.' . . . All the family members are calm because being Soviet workers makes them sure of their future." But all this focus on the individual is accomplished without forgetting the person's place in the community. The individual is always less important than factory, commune, and country. So general views are needed too. The Filippovs in the park show they are not alone in their "joy and happiness."

The broad structure of the story, says the article,

is a rising line because the pace of narration increases from very slow at the beginning to very fast and emotional at the end. The authors of the series attain the necessary effect without any tricks. Viewers after having seen the series are just as sure of the future of the Soviet workers as the Filippovs.

The final picture in the story (a composite) returns the viewer to the emotions at the start.

With the phenomenal success of the Filippov story such projects became mandatory. Rodchenko produced his famous White Sea Canal sequence in 1933, and Markov-Grinberg did his series on Izotov the Donbass miner a year later.

Now and then a blunder would creep into a picture story, and it was pointed out in print to educate photographers and editors. A 1932 *Proletarskoye Foto* article discusses a story entitled "The Factory and Its Builder" in which the featured worker, one Comrade Kalmykov, appears in some shots but not others with a bandaged finger.[32]

Even the Filippov story was seen to have a flaw: the tram in it was shown nearly empty. Since Moscow trams were regularly packed to a point where standing up and breathing were challenges, was this too much to believe? Photography historian Stignaev says, "The majority made themselves believe; it just took a slight shift of consciousness. The minority didn't believe."

Though Mezhericher didn't invent picture stories they may be his greatest legacy. The impact of the approach inspired the editors of *Life* magazine when they started up in 1936 and even reached Roy Stryker eventually. In an April 1940 article in *Survey Graphic* on the photography program of the Farm Security Administration, writer Hartley E. Howe confirmed, "Stryker is coming to think more and more in terms of not one picture but a whole series."

More than sixty years after Mezhericher's prominence came to an end, photographer Yevgeny Khaldei remembered him a little sadly. "He was a lean man with a sickly look about him, " Khaldei said. "A wonderful man. Nothing to look at but when he started to talk about photography he could hypnotize people."

Khaldei, eighteen when he came to TASS for a course in 1935, recalled Mezhericher's downfall two years later: "He was arrested, ruined. I witnessed one episode. I went to the library at the House of Journalists in 1937 and he was standing ahead of me in line, bringing in a book to exchange. The lady found the card, circled that he had returned the book, and told him, 'Comrade Mezhericher, we have instructions not to lend you any more books.' I remember that incident to this day. I witnessed it. That was the year 1937." In the Stalinist system, that poignant, routine moment meant that the leader's fate was sealed.

Khaldei himself knew tragedy before he knew anything else. At the age of one, during a pogrom against the Jews of his Ukrainian village, a bullet went completely through his mother, who was holding him, and lodged in his chest. He not only survived this and then a famine, even eating grass for a time, but grew into an energetic and witty character with a lively imagination that found an outlet in the picture magazines he occasionally saw and avidly read. "*Ogonyuk* [Little Flame] and *Prozhektor* [Searchlight] motivated me toward photography," he said. "I loved the pictures of new cities, kolkhozes [collective farms], and factories."

In a school textbook he stumbled upon a description of how a camera obscura works and realized he could make a camera of his own. He fashioned one out of a cardboard box and his dead grandmother's spectacles, bought sensitized glass plates, and photographed things that didn't require a shutter, that wouldn't move. His first picture, at twelve, was of a nearby Russian Orthodox Church. "I cried later when they blew it up," he said.

His pictures made it into the local newspaper, *Stalin's Worker.* It was easy to predict what the paper would like, housing construction for example, and Khaldei liked that himself. Soon he sent samples of his pictures, glass plates packed into wooden boxes, to the government's photo agency SoyuzFoto in Moscow.

"In 1935 I was invited to Moscow to take a professional development course," he said. "Then I moved there in 1936. It was scary in a way. I came from Donbass in my boots. My grandmother told me not to take my boots off or they would be stolen. I rode the train for 48 hours with my boots on."

At the age of nineteen, Khaldei was working full time in Moscow for SoyuzFoto. He photographed construction of the Moscow subway, and one of his shots made *Pravda's* front page. "I liked industry," he said. "And of course I liked to

Proletarian Foto No. 3, 1932: "Here and Over There: The Photo Post Card As a Bolshevik Information Medium," Author Lazar Mezhericher proposed the production of cards that would show "actual scenes, graphic depictions of the latest living conditions of workers in the nations where capitalism rules." Layouts show:
Upper: The Factory Gates, Ford Plant, Mexico City. The Unemployed Wait in Vain.
Putting a Factory Into Production Is the Greatest Victory.
Lower: Field Maneuvers: Tractor Mounts Are Used for American Artillery Units in the Hawaiian Islands, a US Colony.
Tractors from the Tokarev Plant Are Taking the Fields in the Central Black-Earth Region.

photograph people, since it's people, our people, who create things."

Immediately after Khaldei watched Mezhericher being turned away from the library in 1937, Mezhericher was declared a saboteur and a Trotskyite. The press distributed articles discrediting him. One stated:

The saboteur content of Mezhericher's numerous articles and speeches, though cunningly hidden behind the screen of hurrah-revolutionary phrases, now leaves no doubt about their counter-revolutionary sense. This must be explained to the broad masses of photo workers.[33]

Another article, referring to exhibitions he organized abroad, asked,

Toward who or what did Mezhericher orient photographs as he selected them for the presentation of the Soviet Union abroad? From piles of pictures showing the struggle of collective farmers Mezhericher selected and displayed a casual picture of goslings just because a gosling in the photograph seemed stirring. . . . Such distortions have been employed by the Trotskyist saboteur Mezhericher in his own interests.[34]

Khaldei, who instantly grasped the implications of the Mezhericher library incident, had believed when he was twenty that people like Mezhericher would establish a great Soviet society. He was shocked by the arrest. But the downfall of Mezhericher and others seemed not to have seriously dampened Khaldei's enthusiasm for his work.

Khaldei never joined the Communist Party. Photographers weren't required to and most didn't. But newspaper and magazine editors did join the Party, and they were the ones who bore ultimate responsibility for what was published. Their advance instructions to photographers sometimes were very explicit. "When I was on assignment for the magazine *USSR In Construction*," Markov-Grinberg recalled, "Rodchenko, who did the layout, told me before I went out that it would be good to have such-and-such on the first page, that he would then break the layout into small photographs. Or he would say he needed a large closeup of a worker cropping the harvest. After sketching a detailed plan I would go out to shoot. But anyway we knew what worked well, what would make page one." There were advance layouts but never shooting scripts, never "written instructions" Russians say emphatically.

Always at risk, Soviet editors scrutinized every word and photograph. The Central Committee of the Party perpetually bombarded them with directives of one kind or another. A censoring organization called "Glovlit"—abbreviation for Chief Literary Department—reviewed subjects supposedly having military implications: aerial photos, pictures of railroads, highrises, bridges—these all had to be checked and stamped with approval for publication. (Even through the Gorbachev years every publishing house had a First Department in charge of maintaining secrecy. Precautions included locking up all typewriters before holidays so no one could write anything unauthorized. Moral decency was monitored by the same department.) Generally the mechanism worked. Editors developed a kind of genius for reading the moods and wishes of their bosses, though often enough these skills were not in themselves sufficient to preserve their jobs or their lives.

Despite the oppressive censorship, Soviet editors launched influential magazines. Innovations in printing technologies had opened the way for inexpensive, high-quality photographic reproduction, leading to mass-market illustrated publishing worldwide. A Soviet editor, Mikhail Yefimovich Koltsov was one who foresaw the possibilities for the USSR.

Koltsov was born in 1898 into a family of Kiev craftsmen, took part in the 1917 Bolshevik Revolution, became a *Pravda* correspondent in 1922, and a year later revitalized the languishing *Ogonyuk,* making it into one of the most important Soviet magazines of the era. "The first and main task of the weekly *Ogonyuk,*" wrote Koltsov, "is to inform the wide masses of Soviet Russia with bright and vivid pictures of life and the creative construction of the young republic, and at the same time to convey the feverish, complex tempo of life in the West—class fighting in countries all over the world."[35]

A highly talented organizer, Koltsov went on to establish almost a dozen more magazines, including, *Soviet Foto* (with Rodchenko a member of its first editorial board). In fact, of the three most significant 1930s Soviet magazines the only one Koltsov had nothing to do with was *USSR In Construction*. He had access to every door with power behind it. One of the major posts he held was director of Journalno-Gazetnoye Obedinenije, the Soviet Magazine and Newspaper Association. During the Spanish Civil War he was dispatched to the front as a *Pravda* correspondent but performed duties beyond journalism, obviously working for the NKVD, predecessor to the KGB. Ernest Hemingway mentions Koltsov as a commissar of the Spanish Republican Army in *For Whom the Bell Tolls*.

Back in the USSR after that assignment, Koltsov published a book, *The Spanish Diary*, based on his *Pravda* articles and travel sketches. It was enjoyed by Soviet readers, but Koltsov was arrested in 1938 as an enemy of the people and disappeared into the torture chambers of the NKVD. He was shot in 1939. Today's editor of *Soviet Foto*, Grigory Chudakov, points out that many, like Koltsov, were executed with no specific charges. (Koltsov was "rehabilitated" in 1956–57).

USSR In Construction, intended for foreign readership, debuted in 1930. Writer and editorial board member Maxim Gorky, beloved by the authorities, wrote in the first showy issue,

In order to keep our enemies at home and abroad from belittling the testimony of words and numbers, we have elected to employ the work of light and sun, that of photography. You can't blame the sun for distortion. It gives light to what exists, as it is. . . .[36]

But a short time later he wrote of a more didactic mission: "The goal of our press [in words and photographs] is to reconstruct the old world anew."[37]

Ogonyok No. 27 (537), 25 September 1935 (cover): "Philadelphia (USA): *A Bloody Clash Between Police and 5,000 Striking Workers at a Hosiery Factory*"

USSR In Construction reconstructed the world theatrically. Designers Rodchenko and El Lissitsky wove existing and newly commissioned photography into picture stories and photomontages extolling the regime's accomplishments and projecting utopian visions of the future. On large, lavish pages they staged mythic Socialist Realist epics about building industries, eliminating illiteracy, collectivization, and defense (though this was peacetime). Photography and minimal text were the raw materials of their art, which borrowed freely from film and the stage. Authorship lay with the designer-artists, who collaborated openheartedly with editors and photographers equally idealistic about the powerful blending of content and form. Among other memorable issues designed by Rodchenko was one that featured his remarkably accomplished White Sea Canal photographs. Whether or not the propaganda worked, the world was treated to fresh, daring, imaginative magazine-making, and magazine design was changed forever.

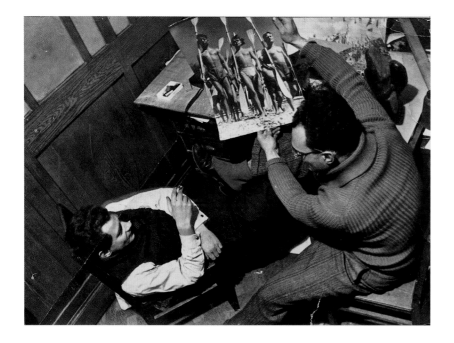

Inexplicably, state terror seems to have been a backdrop that didn't critically diminish enthusiasm or belief. One memory, filtered through friends, comes from then-popular photographer Max Alpert. One day he and two editors were in the magazine's offices sequencing his photographs from a recent assignment. There were so many prints they couldn't evaluate the options from their close vantage point, so the youngest editor climbed on top of a wardrobe where he could see better. Just then Alpert was summoned to the editor-in-chief's office. Saying (and believing) he'd get to a stopping point in a couple of seconds he then proceeded to get so engrossed in the editing that he couldn't tear himself away before the editor-in-chief himself appeared in the doorway, confronting one man hanging off the wardrobe and two huddled intensely over a row of pictures. Trembling, Alpert stammered that he was simply caught up in the creative process. He later recounted the story as a near-death experience, his escape from severe punishment a stroke of extreme good luck.

In terms of energy, idealism, and pure love of photography, Soviet and American photographers were remarkably alike—no doubt talented young people are much the same everywhere—but the paths to getting photographs published in the USA and USSR could not have been more different.

The Soviet effort to get the right pictures published was simply a matter of installing resources and procedures to ensure the desired outcome—after all, the publications, like the photographs, were generated by the government. Extensive publication and dissemination of newspapers, magazines, and posters was the goal. Posters, on buildings, in metro cars, and on specially erected bulletin boards, were an efficient way to get the message out, and the Soviets mastered the form (page 68). The Leningrad school, influenced by European art, tended to be more graphic, colorful, and exciting than the Moscow school—except that Moscow had Rodchenko and his wife Varvara Stepanova.

USSR In Construction, No. 8, 1939
(issue devoted to Soviet women)

USSR In Construction, No. 4, 1937
(issue devoted to Maxim Gorky)

USSR In Construction, No. 4, 1934 (issue devoted to communes for homeless children)

UNKNOWN ARTIST, *The Enemy Is Foreign Intervention!* 1931

YELENA SEMYONOVA, *Rationalize Production and Labor!* 1930

UNKNOWN ARTIST, *Establish a 2nd Coal and Metallurgy Source,* 1930

VASILY YOLKIN, *Let Us Liquidate the Homelessness of Auto Transport,* 1931

VERA GITSEVICH, *Komsomol Members and Pioneers! Breed Rabbits!* 1932

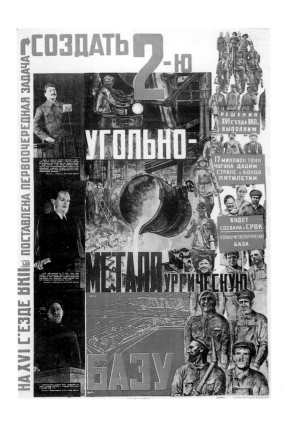

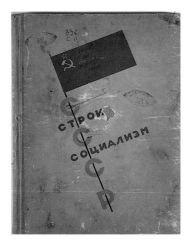

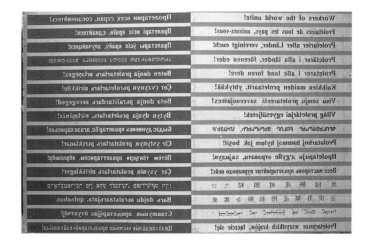

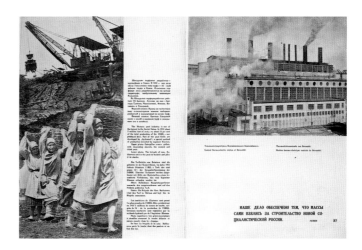

USSR Builds Socialism, book designed by El Lissitsky, published by Izogiz, Moscow, 1933 (cover, endsheets, title page, sample spread)

Designers in both cities sometimes used black-and-white photographs in their posters because they were cheaper than color graphics. In the US, posters were not so key a means of communication as in the USSR, but administrators did hire artists who lovingly produced fine poster advertisements for government programs (page 71).

Unlike newspapers and magazines, Soviet books did not receive wide distribution: Too expensive for the impoverished population, finely designed books by El Lissitsky (above) and Rodchenko praising the regime's accomplishments and sou-

venir albums from factories, army units, and even prison camps honoring those institutions were collectors' items for the privileged.

In the US, proudly independent magazines and newspapers were at first skittish about using government pictures, even very good ones. Related to this was the question of abetting unfair competition between cost-free government photographs and costly independent ones: American editors believed they had to resist any financial enticement that might tempt them to succumb to propaganda. So American

JOHN VACHON, *Newsstand, Omaha, Nebraska*, 1938

Mid-Week Pictorial, July 4, 1936

New York Times Magazine, August 22, 1937 (Gee's Bend article)

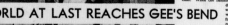

publications often turned down FSA pictures or used them without credit lines.

Internal government publications prepared for aid recipients and the US Congress were merely one avenue of publication for program publicity and photographic pride. These were taken seriously, but were not enough. Fortunately, Stryker, in addition to having an appetite for publishing, turned out to be exceptionally good at breaking down barriers that stood in the way. He built a network that would get FSA photographs into the hands of a wide array of editors, worked to get his photographers credited appropriately, but allowed publication without attribution when it appeared the only option.

The pictorial and socially sensitive magazine *Survey Graphic* became an early and consistent supporter. Before Stryker's Farm Security Administration program even got under way, the magazine had already recognized and published State of California–sponsored pictures by Dorothea Lange and Tennessee Valley Authority pictures by Lewis Hine. In this regard the magazine was exceptional, as FSA expert Jack Hurley pointed out in his 1972 book *Portrait of a*

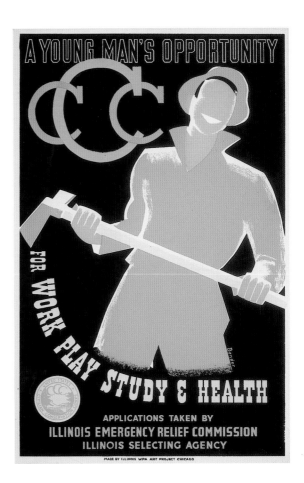

WILFRED J. MEAD, *Civilian Conservation Corps recruit*, undated

ALBERT BENDER, *Chicago Federal Art Project, WPA*, c. 1937

Decade. So *Survey Graphic* became the first mainstream magazine to publish FSA pictures—two by Arthur Rothstein only a few months after the program was launched. Rothstein's pictures of rural poverty were used as the FSA intended, to promote government relief programs. The magazine went on to publish other FSA photographers, along with texts unabashedly sympathetic to Stryker's program.

By 1940 nearly two hundred newspapers and magazines had published FSA photographs, including *Saturday Evening Post, Collier's, Time, Life, Look, Newsweek, McCall's,* and *Current History.* The *New York Times Magazine* was so eager to run an FSA pictorial series on Gee's Bend, Alabama, that a writer was dispatched to do a story to go with the pictures.

But Stryker wanted more. He desired proof that his pictures held up photographically: He wanted the endorsement of the art world. So he went about getting FSA photographs exhibited. He succeeded dramatically, winning places for FSA photographs in a show sponsored by *US Camera* in 1936, then exhibitions for the College Art Association and the Carl Zeiss company, and most significantly the International Photography Exhibition at New York's Grand Central Palace, April 18–19, 1938.

Arthur Rothstein and Russell Lee worked for weeks selecting the approximately seventy pictures for that New York show and having them printed large—some 11 x 14", some as large as 30 x 40". Rothstein thought up the idea of putting out cards for people to use in registering reactions—540 people responded. A sampling of their comments[38] suggests that the photographs generally had the desired effect:

Your pictures demonstrate clearly that one half of the people do not know how the other half lives.

Very terrible, something should be done about it. Foreign countries aren't the only ones. We have it right here.

The pictures are very enlightening. I thought these conditions existed only in the south—certainly never in my home state of Minnesota.

Support Roosevelt's program for farm relief.

Occasionally there was a dissenter:

Subversive propaganda.

Photography exhibitions were also significant events in the Soviet Union. Organizers of a major 1935 show invited a broad range of prospective participants to submit 20 pictures each to a committee that included Mezhericher and Rodchenko. In the resulting display of 400 photographs, so-called formalist images were hung alongside ostensibly straightforward documentary. The show, entitled "Exhibition of Works by the Masters of Soviet Photo Art," took place during a brief interlude in which diverse styles were tolerated or even encouraged. But the terror that descended over all aspects of Soviet life in 1937 put a final end to whatever real artistic discussion was still taking place.

In the USA several classic books have become permanent testaments to FSA accomplishment, and in fact have seemed almost to obliterate the genuine photographic achievement of other New Deal agencies. But the first popular, commercially successful book about rural poverty during the Depression—*You Have Seen Their Faces,* published in 1937—was the non-FSA product of a collaboration by *Fortune* and *Life* photographer Margaret Bourke-White and her husband, best-selling writer Erskine Caldwell. Bourke-White used her subjects as actors and props, rearranged their possessions,

and brought in lighting to suit her dramatic or sculptural needs. Caldwell's text took even more liberties with reality. He writes at the start that his captions are what the authors imagine their subjects to say (opposite).

You Have Seen Their Faces seems exploitative compared to An American Exodus, a book that grew out of the collaboration between Dorothea Lange and her second husband Paul Taylor. Taylor, a professor of labor economics working on rural rehabilitation for the State of California, offers a flat, fact-filled text to accompany the photographs—most but not all of them Lange's—in which the emotion is found. Unlike the effects of Bourke-White's stage management, in Lange's pictures the feeling seems to emanate from the subjects themselves, from their humanity and yearning. Though Lange's creed was to photograph life as it was, without artifice, she controlled her work precisely. She communed with her subjects, worked with them as she saw fit, in ways that reflected her own insights and tastes.

In 1938 Archibald MacLeish paid homage to FSA pictures in his book *Land of the Free* through the unprecedented act of writing poetry to support the photography. Printing his verse on the left-hand pages MacLeish meant the lyrics to be a "sound track," putting words to the pictures on the right and into the mouths of their subjects.

We wonder if the liberty is done:
The dreaming is finished
We can't say
We aren't sure

Or if there's something different men can dream
Or if there's something different men can mean by
Liberty . . .
Or if there's liberty a man can mean that's
Men: not land

We wonder
We don't know
We're asking

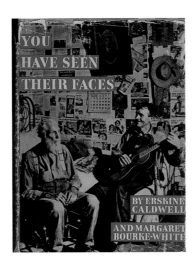
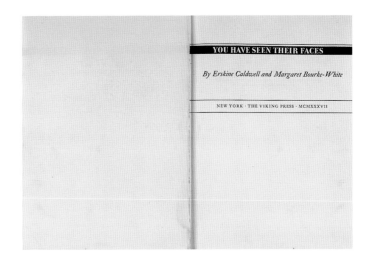
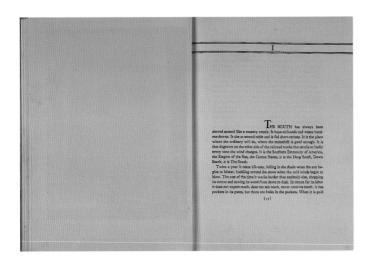
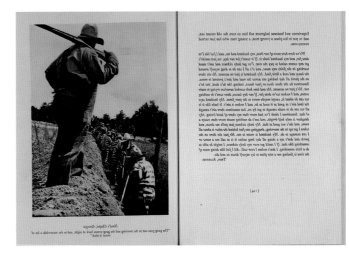
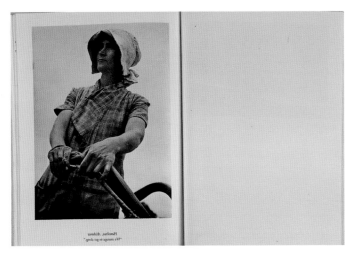

You Have Seen Their Faces, text by Erskine Caldwell and photographs by Margaret Bourke-White, 1937

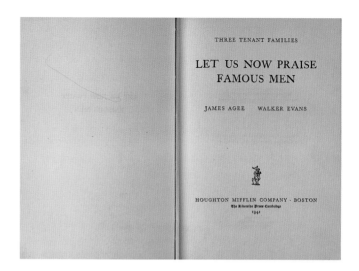

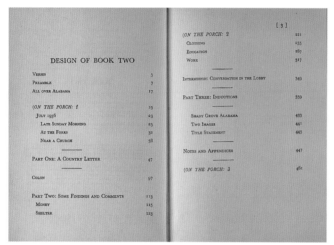

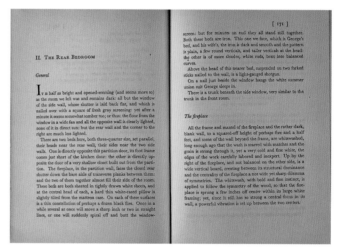

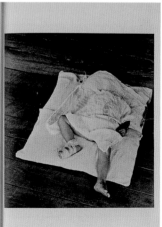

Let Us Now Praise Famous Men, text by James Agee and photographs by Walker Evans, 1941

The text in other books was also respectful of the photography—as in Sherwood Anderson's *Home Town* and Richard Wright's and Edwin Rosskam's *Twelve Million Black Voices* (both 1941). (Rosskam had joined the Historical Section in 1938 to assemble slide shows and traveling exhibitions.)

The year 1941 also saw publication of *Let Us Now Praise Famous Men*, with text by James Agee and photographs by Walker Evans (opposite). The book stirred little interest at the time. It sold poorly (in part because people were already focusing on the war). But it is now named by some scholars as the finest work of the era. The project started in 1936 when *Fortune* assigned James Agee to write an article on cotton tenancy. Agee obtained approval for Evans to do the photography. In the end, *Fortune* rejected Agee's text, which editors considered too negative and personal.

Evans took an eye-level, even-light approach to his pictures. His still lifes and location shots of house fronts, unremarkable rooms, signs, and railroad tracks are presented as found but not as uncontrolled; they resonate with the absent people who live in these settings. Attending to every framing nuance, Evans worked with a tripod. His rigorous, quiet photographs dignified the poverty and monotony he saw by exalting its textural detail—silverware nailed to a wall, an iron bed angled under a shotgun, a washstand under a towel hanging from a nail, a mantel with vases and a calendar. He reacted with horror to the idea of Rothstein's moved skull and Bourke-White's stage-directing and operatic lighting. What sets Evans—and Lange too—apart from Bourke-White is the way they balance control with seeing: their seeing always seems to rise up and ultimately determine the image.

Evans succeeded in really collaborating with his subjects; the Fields and the Burroughs, as individuals and entire families, are not just looked at but are actively encouraged to arrange themselves for their portraits, to be partners in the production of their pictures. The result calls into question the assumed superior documentary authenticity of the candid picture, the chance, stolen, or exploited moment chosen by photographer or editor as the truth of the matter.

Let Us Now Praise Famous Men was completed in 1939 and then rejected by Harper and Brothers, who had agreed to publish it when the project was proposed two years earlier. They balked when Agee demanded that it go forward without editing. It was finally published in September 1941 by Houghton Mifflin.

Agee's text scrupulously documented the material components of his tenants' lives, tried to peel away anything that might put the author between the readers and their literal experience of the subject. And his anguished effort is itself meticulously documented. In his reverence for, intimacy with, and love of his subjects he explores their humanity and also his own.

Agee, like the Soviets, proposed that poor people remained purer, better than those tainted with money; they would, or should be Famous Men. But Soviet and American documentarians portrayed the poor for different audiences. FSA photographs were meant for the middle class. To engage its sympathy, middle-class social values were depicted—devotion to family, self-sufficiency, and individual initiative. Socialist Realist pictures simply went to as many people as possible, and the Soviet values of hard work and devotion to community were uppermost.

THE MECHANICAL NATURE OF PHOTOGRAPHY gave it credibility, but Americans and Soviets didn't rely solely on that. If a document was dull its message couldn't be felt. Both sides thought the style and content of a photograph should serve a social and political purpose, and to do so it should be uplifting in some way. There were methods and approaches for accomplishing this: an unmanipulated, offhand, artless look suggested truth; a composition showing soulful people in grim circumstances elicited sympathy; a heroic angle paid tribute to heroic accomplishment. By keeping themselves invisible photographers implied that their photographs were objective—simply seen and recorded. With rare exception no one in either country thought these ways to photograph lessened the truth-bearing qualities of the results.

But the two countries were also remarkably unalike historically and culturally. The most profound difference—the one that most shaped history—was the relationship between individual and community.

The Russian collective impulse was rooted in village life, rather than Marxism or Communism. It was cultural rather than political, with patriotism and self-sacrifice among the array of expressions it had: The moral Russian individual was called upon to yield unselfishly to his people. Americans on the other hand believed that the individual had a basic right to act aggressively on his own behalf, to make his own future, and each person was responsible for whatever his fate turned out to be. This was good for everybody, the thinking went.

These different values determined how citizens viewed themselves and their governments, what they accepted or questioned. And it influenced what they photographed: Sports parades (metaphors for the Stalin machine in which each person could be controlled and replaced), political rallies, throngs of farmers collectivizing, and work crews building monumental industrial complexes were solely the stuff of Socialist Realism; American construction projects looked like smaller affairs. Rallies, considered formidable rather than favorable events by Americans, rarely occurred in the US at that point, and were even more rarely photographed. The everyday domestic details of life—families at home, social and church activities, individuals working or out of work—touched America most and formed the basic fabric of its photography.

Each side had its icons—an American migrant mother, a weather-beaten farmer, a heroically productive Soviet laborer, a Pioneer girl—to extoll the government programs of the day. Pictures of individual heroes and victims served to humanize the ideologies and agendas of both countries.

A goal of the era was to eliminate barriers among media and between purveyors and consumers of art. And in fact there were no sharp distinctions between creators and audiences in either the USSR or US. Policymakers, publishers, and photographers—all were shapers of, receivers of, and believers in their country's cultural and political outlook. The mechanisms that generated photography and those that led to its publication varied, but the acts of choosing, cropping, sequencing, and captioning pictures always expressed the shifting views and served the complex agendas of participants in the process. The material world was revised by layer upon layer of editing (just as it is today).

During that unique period of the post-avant-garde, pre–World War II documentary, photographers from both countries engaged enthusiastically with the life before them, grappled with national themes, and recorded enduring human qualities. But within a few years, the glow of idealism dimmed, the photographers were no longer so young, and their output slowed. Rodchenko was probably inhibited by the condemnation he endured. But Mark Markov-Grinberg, Max Alpert, and Arkady Shaikhet—unrepudiated—also produced less with time. Marion Post Wolcott may have continued to photograph had her husband approved, but Dorothea Lange, with her husband's lifelong support, and Walker Evans, with ever-increasing recognition, were never to surpass their work of the 1930s.

The photographs handed down to us as two separate collections reported two different realities and two perceptions of those realities: The Soviet pictures, tight, cool, heroically composed, indicated that the state endows health, vitality, and productivity and invite the viewer to believe and participate. The American pictures, more intimate and offhand, seemed to show the plight of individuals temporarily down on their luck, inviting better-off viewers to be moved to help. But ultimately these photographs are as enigmatic as the people they portray and the photographers who took them.

WALKER EVANS, *Bud Fields and his family at home, Hale County, Alabama*, 1936

THE USSR: A PORTFOLIO

VIKTOR BULLA, *Pioneers in defense drill, Leningrad,* 1937

BORIS IGNATOVICH, *Band in Red Square, Moscow*, 1927

BORIS IGNATOVICH, *Rally in Red Square, Moscow*, 1935

Upper: IVAN SHAGIN, *Sports parade, Red Square, Moscow,* 1932
Lower: GEORGY ZELMA, *Physical culture demonstration, Red Square,* mid-1930s

ALEXANDER RODCHENKO, *The jump*, 1934

GEORGY ZELMA, *Gorky Park, Moscow,* 1930

Boris Ignatovich, *St. Isaac's Cathedral, Leningrad,* 1930

Upper: Boris Ignatovich, *Stalin with Mamlakat, record-breaking cotton picker,* 1935
Lower: Boris Ignatovich, *Nikita Khrushchev, Secretary of the Moscow City Party Committee,* c. 1936

Max Alpert, *Elections to the USSR Supreme Soviet*, 1936

BORIS IGNATOVICH, *Chess tournament,* 1930s

AMURSKY, *A little tots' playroom in Moscow School number 545*, April 1938

Boris Ignatovich, *Boris Pasternak and Kornei Chukovsky*, 1935

Upper: YAKOV KHALIP, *In the Moscow radio studio,* November 1934
Lower: UNKNOWN PHOTOGRAPHER, *Comrades Court, collective farm, Central Asia,* 1931

MAX PENSON, *Target practice*, 1931–32

DMITRI DEBABOV, *Icons*, 1934

Nikolai Kuleshov, *Untitled (dead duck)*, 1938

Unknown Photographer, *Display against fascism, Obvodny Canal, Leningrad,* 1930s

Upper: BORIS IGNATOVICH, *Maternity,* 1937
Lower: GEORGY PETRUSOV, *Dinner in the Kolkhoz field, Ukraine,* 1934

DMITRI DEBABOV, *Hunter with golden eagle, Kazakhstan*, 1935

Upper: MARK MARKOV-GRINBERG, *Happy Maternity, Stavropol Territory*, 1935
Left: YEVGENY KHALDEI, *Construction worker, Dnepr-Bug Canal*, 1940

ARKADY SHISHKIN, *Gleaning,* 1932

Upper: UNKNOWN PHOTOGRAPHER, *First-year students preparing for exams, Moscow,* 1937
Lower: GEORGY PETRUSOV, *Mobile library in the Kolkhoz, Ukraine,* 1934

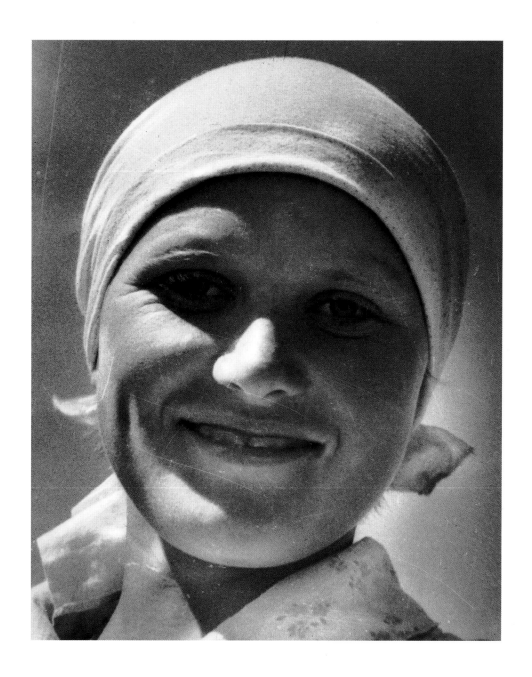

ARKADY SHISHKIN, *Gleaning*, 1932

MAX ALPERT, *Magnitogorsk metallurgical plant construction site, Urals*, 1929

MAX ALPERT, *Construction of the Fergana Canal*, 1939

GEORGY PETRUSOV, *Magnitogorsk furnace*, 1930

Boris Ignatovich, *Furnace (steel casting)*, 1937

Boris Ignatovich, *Workers*, 1930

Upper and Lower: LEONID SHOKIN, *From the series* Manufacture of Felt Boots, *Kimry,* 1930s

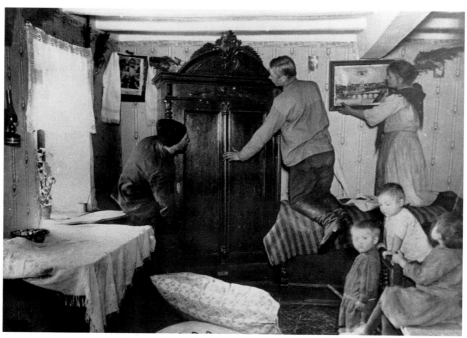

Upper: Dmitri Debabov, *"We shall enter new factory workshops armed with the six historic directives of Comrade Stalin," Magnitogorsk, Urals,* 1930
Lower: Max Alpert, *A Kulak's cottage is given to a poor peasant,* 1930

Mark Markov-Grinberg, *Public letter to a slacker from record-breaking collective farmers, Stalingrad Region*, 1933

GEORGY ZELMA, *Phonograph demonstration, Central Asia,* 1935–37

DMITRI DEBABOV, *Concert in Chukotka*, 1936

Georgy Lipskerov, *The Last Veil*, 1932

DMITRI DEBABOV, *Rugmaking, Armenia,* 1940

GEORGY ZELMA, *Caviar, Astrakhan*, 1931–35

DMITRI DEBABOV, *Hundred-year-old pike, Olkhon Island, Lake Baikal*, 1938

GEORGY LIPSKEROV, *The jump of Lyuba Berlin*, 1935

M. Ostrekin, *USSR N-169 Aircraft expedition into the northern latitudes*, 1941

Upper: ARKADY SHAIKHET, *Fisherman, Caspian Sea,* 1932
Lower: YAKOV KHALIP, *Guard, Kronstadt, Baltics,* 1936

SERGEI STRUNNIKOV, *First ice floe (from the mast of the icebreaker Krasin), Karsk Sea*, 1934

VIKTOR TEMIN, *Moscow welcomes the Chelyuskin survivors*, 1934

Boris Ignatovich, *Strastnoy Boulevard, Moscow*, 1930s

GEORGY PETRUSOV, *New building*, 1928–30

ELIZAR LANGMAN, *Old lifestyle around the Dinamo factory*, 1930

Upper: Elizar Langman, *Workers writing*, 1930
Lower: Elizar Langman, *Kindergarten*, 1930

Elizar Langman, *Fighting for bread*, 1930

ELIZAR LANGMAN, *Youth commune Dinamo at morning tea*, 1930

Unknown Photographer, *Cedar of Lebanon at Massandra Spa, Crimea*, 1938

Upper: Ivan Shagin, *The first passengers: builders of the Metro, Moscow,* 1935
Lower: Unknown Photographer, *Children's movie in a village clubhouse, Leningrad vicinity,* 1930s

Georgy Zelma, *Moscow,* 1931

Olga Ignatovich, *Dinamo vs. Spartak soccer match*, 1940

ALEXANDER GRINBERG, *Untitled (acrobat)*, 1930s

ALEXANDER GRINBERG, *A dance routine,* early 1930s

L. SMIRNOV, *Park of Culture and Recreation, Moscow,* 1938

Unknown Photographer, *Woman applying lipstick*, early 1930s

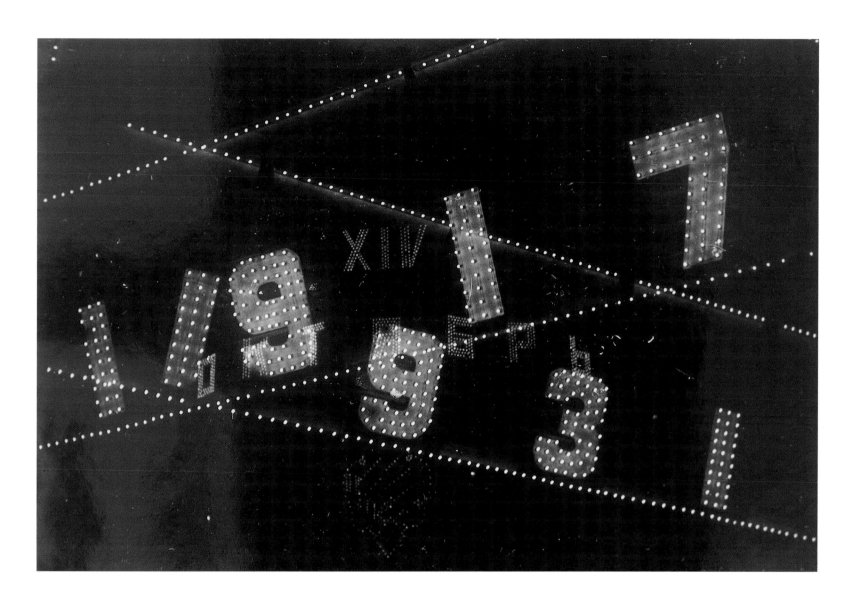

Nikolai Kuleshov, *Untitled (Moscow)*, 1931

OLEG KNORING, *Untitled (woman collective farmer), Voronezh Region,* 1938

ARKADY SHAIKHET, *Field lighting, Moscow Region,* 1936

BORIS IGNATOVICH, *Factory*, 1930s

Left: MARK MARKOV-GRINBERG, *Lowering the double-headed eagle from the Kremlin towers, Moscow,* 1935
Right: MARK MARKOV-GRINBERG, *Raising the five-pointed star on Spasskaya Tower of the Kremlin, Moscow,* 1935

ALEXANDER RODCHENKO, *The Orchestra, White Sea Canal*, 1933

BORIS IGNATOVICH, *Near the Hermitage,* 1930

THE US: A PORTFOLIO

DOROTHEA LANGE, *Ditched, stalled, and stranded couple inside car, San Joaquin, California,* 1935

DOROTHEA LANGE, *US 54, north of El Paso, Texas, one of the westward routes of the migrants,* 1938

Arthur Rothstein, *Tenant farmer moving his household goods to a new farm, Hamilton County, Tennessee,* 1937

DOROTHEA LANGE, *Migrant workers camp, Marysville Vicinity, California,* 1935

ARTHUR ROTHSTEIN, *The family of migrating fruit worker from Tennessee now camped in a field near the packing house at Winterhaven, Florida,* 1937

DOROTHEA LANGE, *Lunchtime for cotton hoers, Mississippi Delta*, 1937

ARTHUR ROTHSTEIN, *Alleta Bendolf in log cabin, Gee's Bend, Alabama,* 1937

Russell Lee, *Abandoned theater decorated with bottle caps, Quemado, Texas,* 1939

ARTHUR ROTHSTEIN, *Room where migratory agricultural workers sleep, Camden County, New Jersey,* 1938

Upper: GORDON PARKS, *Ella Watson, a government charwoman leaves for work at 4:30 pm, Washington, DC,* 1942
Lower: GORDON PARKS, *Ella Watson, US government charwoman, Washington, DC,* 1942

GORDON PARKS, *Mrs. Ella Watson, government charwoman with three grandchildren and adopted daughter, Washington, DC,* 1942

Gordon Parks, *Reverend Gassaway in a bowl of sacred water, Washington, DC*, 1942

ARTHUR ROTHSTEIN, *John Dudeck, an old bachelor living on a sub-marginal farm, Dalton, Allegany County, New York,* 1937

BEN SHAHN, *Street, Murfreesboro, Tennessee*, 1935

Both: MARION POST WOLCOTT, *Sunday afternoon, New Orleans, Louisiana,* 1941

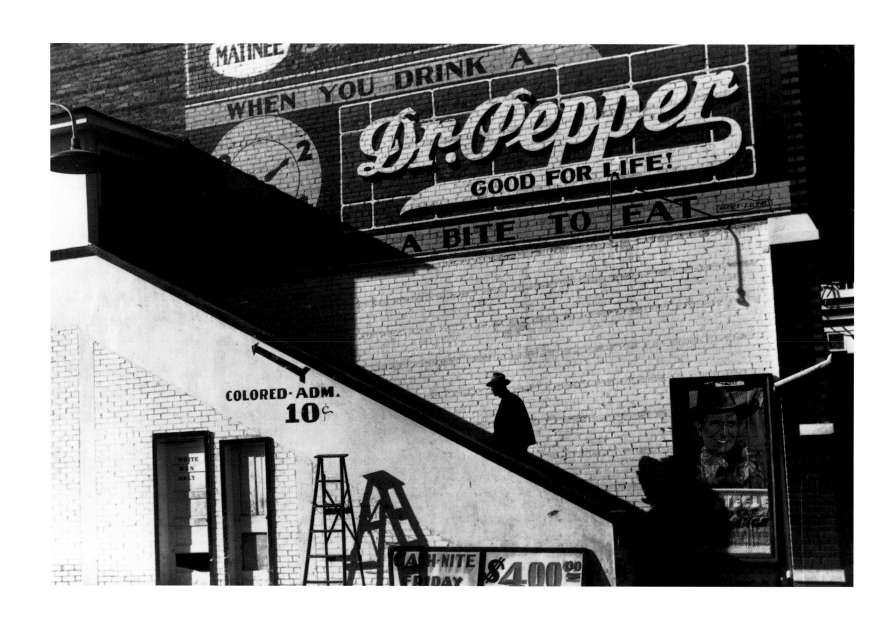

MARION POST WOLCOTT, *Negro going in a colored entrance to movie house on Saturday afternoon, Belzoni, Mississippi,* 1939

JACK DELANO, *In a working class section, Pittsburgh, Pennsylvania,* 1941

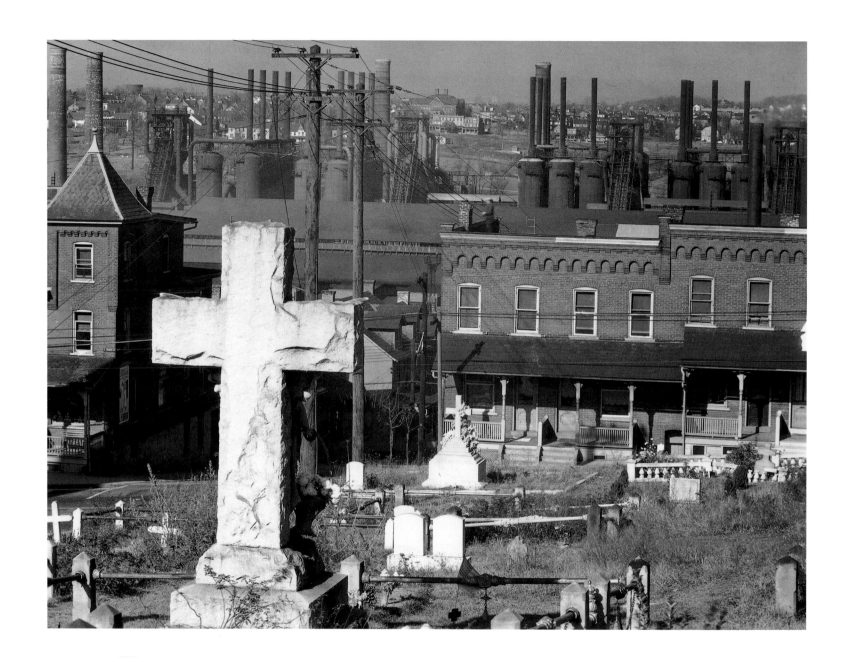

WALKER EVANS, *Bethlehem graveyard and steel mill, Bethlehem, Pennsylvania,* 1935

JACK DELANO, *Houseboat along Ohio River, Rochester, Pennsylvania*, 1941

MARJORY COLLINS, *Minister's daughter sitting on a tombstone watching people come to All Faith Church where her father is a minister, St. Mary's County, Maryland,* 1942

JACK DELANO, *A Negro graveyard on abandoned land in the military reservation areas, Moncks Corner Vicinity, South Carolina*, 1941

Arthur Rothstein, *Steam shovels, Cherokee County, Kansas*, 1936

Arthur Rothstein, *WPA river front improvement project, St. Louis, Missouri,* 1939

RUSSELL LEE, *Sign, Pinal County, Arizona*, 1942

MARION POST WOLCOTT, *Typical Florida road and country, near Winter Haven, Florida*, 1939

BEN SHAHN, *Repairing US Highway 40, Central Ohio*, 1938

ARTHUR ROTHSTEIN, *Coming out of the mine, Birmingham, Alabama,* 1937

JACK DELANO, *Inside Kenyon's Johnny Cake Flour Mill, Usquepaugh, Rhode Island*, 1940

Upper: Marion Post Wolcott, *Coal miner in his home, a company house, Pursglove, Scott's Run, West Virginia,* 1938
Lower: Russell Lee, *Pushing a car load of gold ore along track in mine, Mogollon, New Mexico,* 1940

Russell Lee, *Children taking a bath in their home in community camp, Oklahoma City, Oklahoma,* 1939

Marion Post Wolcott, *Why open the door? Coal miner's child uses the "cat hole," Bertha Hill, West Virginia*, 1938

JACK DELANO, *Family living in the "Crackerbox" slum tenement, Beaver Falls, Pennsylvania,* 1941

JACK DELANO, *The Family of FSA client Peter V. Andrews, Portuguese. They run a small 7-acre vegetable farm, near Falmouth, Massachusetts,* 1940

Carl Mydans, *Bed and sitting room, Hamilton, Ohio,* 1935

RUSSELL LEE, *Tenant purchase clients at home, Hidalgo County, Texas,* 1939

Arthur Rothstein, *Farmer and sons walking in the face of a dust storm, Cimarron County, Oklahoma*, 1936

Arthur Rothstein, *Rural scene, Keota, Colorado,* 1939

DOROTHEA LANGE, *Power farming displaces tenants from the land in the western dry cotton area, Childress County, Texas Panhandle*, 1938

DOROTHEA LANGE, *Hop harvesting, Wheatland, California*, 1935

JACK DELANO, *View of the sea town of Stonington, Connecticut,* 1940

Dorothea Lange, *Family farmstead, Nebraska*, 1940

Unknown Photographer, *FSA-sponsored "Know Your Farmer" Tour stops at home of tenant purchase borrower, Lowndes County, Mississippi,* 1940

Marion Post Wolcott, *Brunswick stew dinner in front of the tobacco warehouse on opening day of the auctions, Mebane, North Carolina*, 1940

JACK DELANO, *Spectators at the Champlain Valley Exposition, Essex Junction, Vermont*, 1941

Esther Bubley, *A house as seen from window of a Greyhound Bus, Gettysburg, Pennsylvania,* 1943

JACK DELANO, *Special agent making his rounds at night at the South Water Street Freight Terminal of the Illinois Central Railroad, Chicago, Illinois,* 1943

ARTHUR SIEGEL, *A traffic control island around which the traffic moves in several directions, Detroit, Michigan*, 1942

WALKER EVANS, *Scott's Run mining camps, domestic interior, shack at Osage, near Morgantown, West Virginia,* 1935

WALKER EVANS, *61st Street between 1st and 3rd Avenues, children playing in the street, New York*, 1938

DOROTHEA LANGE, *Drought farmers line the shady side of the main street of the town while their crops burn up in the fields, Sallisaw, Sequoyah County, Oklahoma,* 1936

Ben Shahn, *Medicine show, Huntington, Tennessee,* 1935

Upper: ARTHUR ROTHSTEIN, *Farmers in town, Fairfield, Montana,* 1939
Lower: JOHN VACHON, *Business section, Dubuque, Iowa,* 1940

WALKER EVANS, *Street, Vicksburg, Mississippi,* 1936

Russell Lee, *Ride at the carnival which was part of the Fourth of July celebration, Vale, Oregon*, 1941

Upper: RUSSELL LEE, *Princesses, National Rice Festival, Crowley, Louisiana,* 1938
Lower: MARION POST WOLCOTT, *A woman sunning, Miami Beach, Florida,* 1939

JACK DELANO, *Movies in the school auditorium in Centralhatchee, Heard County, Georgia*, 1941

RUSSEL LEE, *Cajun Band Contest, National Rice Festival, Crowley, Louisiana,* 1938

Theodor Jung, *Sunday dinner, Jackson, Ohio,* 1936

JOHN VACHON, *Girl and movie poster, Cincinnati, Ohio,* 1938

RUSSELL LEE, *Round dance. Among people where square dancing is the usual form of dancing, regular ball dancing is called "round dancing," Pie Town, New Mexico*, 1940

ARTHUR ROTHSTEIN, *Cotton Carnival, hog calling contest, Hayti, Missouri*, 1942

RUSSELL LEE, *Spanish-American acrobat of traveling show, Penasco, New Mexico,* 1940

ARTHUR ROTHSTEIN, *Farm people at Central Iowa Fair, Marshalltown, Iowa*, 1939

WALKER EVANS, *Minstrel (circus) poster in Alabama town*, 1936

WALKER EVANS, *Photographer's window of penny portraits, Birmingham, Alabama,* 1936

ANDREAS FEININGER, *Executives who keep heavy ore production coming from the open-pit mines of the Utah Copper Company looking out over the mine workings, Bingham Canyon, Utah*, 1942

ARTHUR ROTHSTEIN, *Steel workers, Aliquippa, Pennsylvania,* 1938

DOROTHEA LANGE, *One of Chris Adolf's younger children, FSA rehabilitation clients, Near Wapoto, Yakima Valley, Washington,* 1939

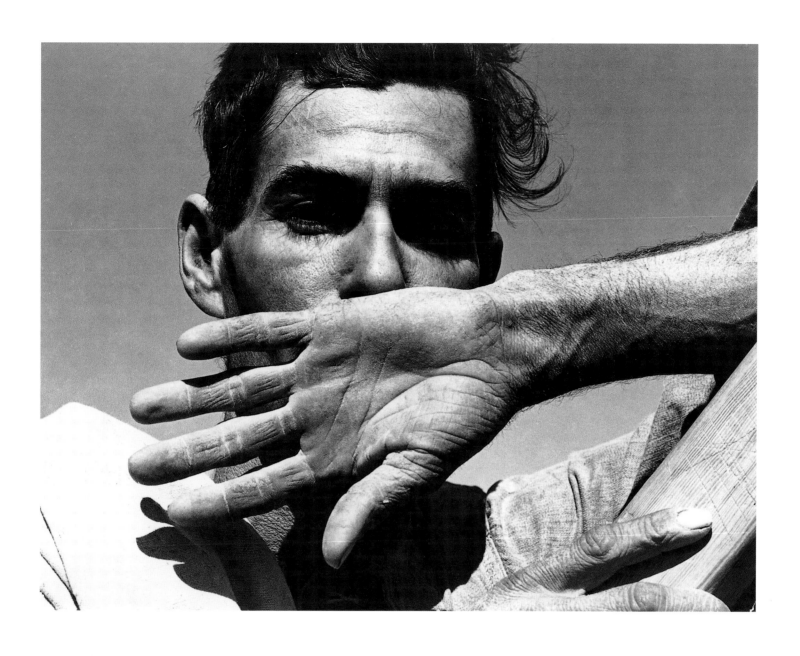

DOROTHEA LANGE, *Migratory cotton picker, Eloy, Arizona,* 1940

AFTERWORD

LOOKING BACK ON THE VISUAL CULTURE OF THE 1930S from the kind of postmodern vantage we easily adopt today, a new picture of our history emerges. We do not see a unified image, however. What we see is like a jigsaw puzzle constructed of many interlocking fragments. Each tiny piece does not tell the whole truth about the past. Photography never does.

Yet, laid out together and studied from the distance of reasoned time, these pieces do add up to something approximating real history. It is a history of relationships, between opposing political ideologies, between creative artists and governments struggling to define themselves, and between a tattered truth and fictional representation, coexisting without either taking precedence.

Since many of the images in *Propaganda & Dreams* were made with an underlying political agenda, they hold within them the seeds of artistic as well as political revolutions. America's Farm Security Administration photographers redefined the art of documentary image-making for generations to follow. The clarity of their visions and their collective ability to generate hard-hitting narratives from the stuff of the Great Depression certainly parallels, and is informed by, the storytelling strategies of Soviet filmmakers during these years. Soviet photographers were also constructing with images the hopes and goals of their then young nation. While their work was more dispersed and the creative,

experimental passion that dominated Soviet arts and design in the twenties was by then mediated, their stylized portrayal of the thirties reminds us now of the histrionic nature of everyday life.

It is this tension between realism and the theatrical constructs of photographers in both the Soviet Union and the United States that warrants another look today. The photographs are inherently real. They picture what the photographers saw, whether found or staged. Editing, printing, and the context of their presentation also manipulate our perception of events. Such artifice not only brings the images to life, animating them and helping us imagine the singular importance of an unspoken government presence, but it also creates a metaphorical stage, which in turn connects real images from the thirties to past and future mythologies.

In some ways, our ability to create and interpret documentary images in multiple ways has significantly changed since the 1930s. Our visual language has been transformed because the illusion of photography has become commonplace and its multiplicity compromised. Technology and the immediacy of the medium itself have diluted the magic connection between an artist's subject and the photographic object. While images still provide evidence, beauty, and often heart-stopping emotions, bits of history sliced from those same politicized fields photographed by Walker Evans, Alexander Rodchenko, Dorothea Lange, and Boris Ignatovich, they now come to us live by satellite from remote rooftops, complete with real-time live commentary by witnesses. It is easier now to question our eyes and ears in the field.

The modern influence of 1930s documentary processes on contemporary photographers is more about form than content. It is about searching for a form that seems true. Today we must reference the inauthentic nature of the documentary image in order to seek its authenticity. And in doing so we are searching for proof of photography's dual meanings. On one hand, photographs measure the world, reproducing it factually like a mirror to create proof or evidence of something that happened in front of the photographer's lens. On the other, photographs abstract real time and space, compressing what really happened, like a shadow, into a metaphorical syntax of its own. These are parallel languages of evidence and metaphor, truth and fiction.

The combination of documentary pictures with fabricated ideals represents the equivocal notion of truth in a variety of ways. Photographs may be staged or set up or they may be exact representations of historical events. They may use archives, texts, or props to build alternative views of history that question the relationship between truth and fiction. Scanning the archives of Soviet and American photography in the 1930s, we now rediscover a language that both preserves and alters our view of history because both memory and history strongly depend on such ambiguous representations. These images construct both propaganda and dreams, for photographs, like memories, represent an illusion of the real world rather than the world itself.

PHILIP BROOKMAN
The Corcoran Gallery of Art

USSR

Max Alpert was born in Simferopol in the Crimea in 1899, the son of an artisan. At fifteen he went to Odessa and was apprenticed to a photographer. He volunteered for the Red Army in 1919, then joined the Moscow newspaper *Rabochaya Gazeta* after his demobilization in 1924. *Pravda* hired him four years later and, on assignment, he photographed the collectivization of agriculture and construction during the first Five Year Plan. Beginning in 1931 he worked for the prestigious magazine *USSR In Construction* on stories meant for foreign consumption. He covered the digging of the Fergana Canal in epic style and, together with Arkady Shaikhet and Salomon Tules, created the picture story titled "Twenty-Four Hours in the Life of the Filippov Family." This story about a worker in Moscow's Red Proletarian factory was published in the German weekly *Arbeiter Illustrierte Zeitung* and established the photo essay as an important photographic genre. During World War II Alpert reported for TASS. Afterward he worked for the Soviet Information Office and Novosti Press Agency. Throughout his career he declared himself against the artificial staging of photographs and was an advocate of the appearance of photographic straightforwardness. He died in 1980.

Viktor Bulla, born in 1883, learned photography in his father's renowned St. Petersburg studio. The young Bulla first published his own pictures (of the 1904–5 Russo-Japanese War) in the local magazine *Niva*. He documented the Revolution and, immediately following that, the authorities appointed him head of the family studio. He photographed Lenin and recorded many official scenes and events but was restless, without ideological passion, and throughout the 1920s and 1930s he roved St. Petersburg photographing, in straightforward style, nearly everything he saw. In 1937 he was shot for unspecified reasons. Though executions were common, photographers were rarely targeted. It may be that he recorded too much, or involved himself in politically unsavory associations.

Dmitri Debabov was born in the village of Kontche'yevo near Moscow on November 4, 1899. While a youth he worked as a machinist in a metalworking plant. He then became a fine arts painter and went on to study drama and film and met the famous director Sergei Eisenstein. It was Eisenstein who urged Debabov to take up photography. The magazine *Sovetskoye Foto* published one of Debabov's early pictures, and this led to a job at the newspaper *Izvestia* in 1926. His career took off. Carrying his Leica and traveling by train, dogsled, automobile, and boat, Debabov took pictures throughout the USSR—in the Urals, in Armenia, in northwest Siberia, and into the Arctic. He photographed mining and manufacturing, whaling and icebreaking expeditions, and the inhabitants and wild scenery of the Soviet Union's remotest regions. Debabov died in 1949 from complications during surgery. His son, three years old at the time, believes his father was murdered. Several of Debabov's colleagues, now in their eighties and nineties, disagree.

Alexander Grinberg was born in Moscow in 1885. He witnessed the turmoil leading to the Revolution and lived long enough to see most of the cataclysmic upheavals resulting from it. He took up photography at age ten and joined the Russian Photographic Society at age twenty-two. In 1914 he began working as a cinematographer, but this was soon interrupted when he was sent to fight in the First World War. After the war he went to the Odessa Film Factory where he resumed his filmwork as a cameraman. He taught, made films, served in a variety of administrative posts, and photographed into old age. He died in 1979.

Boris Ignatovich, born April 4, 1899, in the Ukrainian city of Lutzk, began working as a journalist at age nineteen. He took up photography when he received a Kodak camera as a gift five years later. His first pictures were of post-Revolution changes in the Ukraine and showed construction, industrialization, and agriculture. During the 1930s he was the first Soviet photographer to make aerials. He befriended Alexander Rodchenko, was influenced by him, and joined the avant-garde art organization Oktober, even leading the group briefly when Rodchenko was expelled in 1931. He dabbled in documentary filmmaking between 1930 and 1932, had his pictures published in a variety of publications including *Ogonyok* and *USSR In Construction,* and showed his work in exhibitions. In a stint as head of Soyuzfoto he brought photojournalists (including his wife Yelizaveta and his sister Olga) together in his high-spirited "Ignatovich Brigade." The newspaper pictures they published were credited "Ignatovich Brigade Photo," with no indication of individual photojournalist. Ignatovich was one of the few photographers who joined the Communist Party. He was criticized and temporarily expelled from the Party during the 1920s because of his non-conformity, specifically his use of photographic devices like foreshortening and tilted perspectives. He was highly productive, but much of his work went unpublished during his lifetime. He died in Moscow in 1976.

Olga Ignatovich, born in 1905, learned photography from her older brother Boris. She began photographing early in the 1930s and joined the "Ignatovich Brigade" at Soyuzfoto. Her photographs, with sharp differences of scale between foreground and background, often captured active relationships among her subjects. Ignatovich was one of the very few women who went on to photograph on the front lines during World War II. Afterward she worked for the Novosti Press Agency and the Soviet Artist Publishing House. She died in 1984.

Yevgeny Khaldei was born on March 10, 1917 in the town of Yuzovka (later called Stalino and now Donetsk) in the Ukraine. From his home town he followed and admired pictures by Dmitri Debabov, Arkady Shaikhet, Max Alpert, and others who were successfully working in the capital. "There was no opportunity to see photojournalism done outside the USSR in the thirties," Khaldei said. In 1935, having photographed diligently as a hobby and for local newspapers for three years, he sent a selection of glass plate negatives, carefully packaged in wooden boxes, to Soyuzfoto in Moscow and was invited to take a photography course. "I was full of enthusiasm and nothing besides," he recalled. Max Alpert, one of his teachers, was almost an idol. Success came easily to Khaldei—he understood what the regime needed. "It was the fashion to take pictures in a monumental way," he said. "And anyway there was a sort of photographic crisis. The demand was high, so everything I shot was published." He graduated from glass plates and a 9x12cm photoCor camera to a Leica, and with it made his most famous photographs during World War II. Unlike other Soviet photographers of the time he was never drawn to cinematography. After the war he returned to Moscow, married, raised two children, and continued photographing. He died in 1997 at the age of eighty.

YAKOV KHALIP was born in 1908 into a theatrical family in St. Petersburg. From there he moved to Moscow at age thirteen. In the mid-1920s he studied cinematography and began to take photographs. He worked in cinematography until 1931, then devoted himself exclusively to still photography. Like Khaldei he found inspiration in pictures by Rodchenko, Shaikhet, and Alpert. In 1936 he photographed the navy at Kronstadt to illustrate a book. Photographer Vladislav Mikosha also worked on the project, and there was controversy over just who had taken some of the pictures. In 1938 on a North Pole expedition, Khalip photographed a research station as it drifted on an ice floe. From 1938 until 1941 he worked for *USSR In Construction,* then, during the war, went to the front. Afterward he worked for *Ogonyok* and other magazines. He died in 1980.

OLEG KNORING was born in 1907 and became a photographer at the beginning of the 1930s. His early work was published in *Our Achievements* magazine. During World War II he photographed on the front lines, and in the postwar years he worked for *Ogonyok* magazine. He died in 1968.

ELIZAR LANGMAN was born in Odessa in 1935. Not certain of what profession he wished to pursue, he studied at the Odessa Art School, the Kharkov Polytechnical Institute, and the Moscow Conservatory, where he took up the violin. He came to photography late, after performing in musical ensembles, working as an emergency crew chief for a railroad, assisting the architect who designed Moscow's Dinamo stadium, designing posters, and doing publications layouts. As a photographer he joined the avant-garde Oktober group, considered himself a disciple of Rodchenko, and worked in the Ignatovich Brigade. His photographs combined sharp diagonals and foreshortening with a distinctive humanism. He was considered a leftist and a formalist and on these grounds was often selected as an example for criticism in photographic publications. Though his photography career was relatively short—less than twenty years—he was known, written about, and held in high esteem. He died in 1939.

GEORGY LIPSKEROV was born into a wealthy Moscow family on August 16, 1896. His father, who had made his fortune betting on horses, owned the Detgeis Publishing House, which published the popular *News of the Day*. Lipskerov loved sports and adventure travel and he took up photography as a hobby to photograph his interests. In 1918 he volunteered for the Red Army and was assigned to teach physical education to recruits. Afterward, from 1923 to 1931, he worked in various physical culture organizations in Moscow. Midway through that period, in 1927, he had begun to take on extra jobs photographing for newspapers and magazines. When he had a chance to travel on an expedition to the Pamirs in 1931 he purchased a secondhand Leica. At the end of the expedition in 1933 he decided to be a full-time photojournalist. He worked primarily for *Izvestia* until he retired, traveling widely to the Far East and to northern outposts. He died in 1977.

MARK MARKOV-GRINBERG, born November 27, 1907, in Rostov-on-Don, took up photography in secondary school when a friend of his who had a basement darkroom introduced him to the mysteries and joys of his new hobby. In 1925 he landed his first photography job as a stringer for the newspaper *Soviet South*. Between assignments he took the entrance exams for the All-Union Institute of Cinematography, scored high marks, but was rejected "because," he said, "proletarians were preferred. I was a white-collar worker so I became a reporter." In 1926 he left Rostov for Moscow and at first freelanced for several trade union newspapers. In 1929 he accepted an offer from TASS and was given a heavy Nettel 9x12cm camera. "I walked around like a mailman," he recalled, "carrying that Nettel, 24 pieces of glass, and the camera stand, bent to one side with one shoulder up and one down." Eventually Markov-Grinberg's photographs were published in all the Soviet Union's major newspapers and magazines, including the touted *USSR In Construction*. In 1931 he began to use a Leica but, following habits acquired in using glass plates and influenced by limited photographic supplies, he always took only a couple of frames of any situation. Whenever he produced two similar negatives he turned one in and kept one for himself. During World War II Markov-Grinberg's wife, who was evacuated to Siberia for three years, took her husband's negatives with her and saved them.

VLADISLAV MIKOSHA was born on December 8, 1909, in the city of Saratov. After studying at the State Institute of Cinematography he worked for Soyuzkino Chronicle, argued with the director, and was fired. "I was too independent," he says. "After that I exchanged my motion picture camera for a still photography camera." Between 1936 and 1939 Mikosha worked for the newspapers *Izvestia, Pravda,* and *Komsomolskaya Pravda* and the magazines *Ogonyok* and *Soviet Foto* magazines. He photographed industrialization, village life, culture, and sports. But nothing prepared him for the trauma of filming the dynamiting of Moscow's Cathedral of Christ the Savior. His dramatic pictures of this event were published for the first time (in Russia) at the end of the 1980s. In addition to his official assignments, Mikosha worked on personal projects, including a set of postcards on Crimean health resorts and another set on the Black

Sea Navy Fleet. He also participated in producing the first color series of Soviet postage stamps—seventeen of them entitled "The Exhibition of Agricultural Achievements."

MAX PENSON was born in 1893 in the Belorussian village of Velizh. After finishing art school, he fled from anti-Jewish pogroms to Uzbekistan and found a teaching job in Tashkent. In 1921, when he was twenty-eight, he won a camera as a teaching award. He learned to photograph on the street, quit teaching, and began to work for the Russfoto agency and *Pravda Vostoka* (Truth of the East) newspaper, the largest in Central Asia. For two decades he documented Uzbek emergence from tradition to mechanization, from living in tents and wearing veils to driving tractors and learning to read. In the 1940s he was accused of pursuing Western aesthetic styles. He was fired from *Pravda Vostoka* in 1948 after 25 years of service. He died in despair and poverty in 1959.

GEORGY PETRUSOV was born in 1903 in Rostov-on-Don. He took up photography as a hobby while employed in his first job as a book-keeper in a bank. He moved to Moscow in 1924 and from then on worked in photography full-time, initially for two trade union magazines, then for *Pravda*. From 1928 to 1930 he was chief of the information department at Magnitogorsk Steelworks and documented its construction from foundation to the opening of the first blast furnace. From 1930 until the beginning of World War II Petrusov photographed a wide variety of subjects for *USSR In Construction*. During the war he took pictures at the front, then continued to work on illustrated magazines. He died in 1971.

ALEXANDER RODCHENKO was born in St. Petersburg on November 23, 1891. From 1910 to 1914 he attended art school in Kazan where he met his future wife Varvara Stepanova. In 1915 he moved to Moscow to the Stroganov Academy of Decorative Arts. He used photography at first simply to record his paintings, but then, in 1923, he began to experiment with photomontage. He made portraits of family and friends, including a famous series on the poet Mayakovsky. Rodchenko's search for artistic forms that could express the Soviet Union's new political and social realities led him to try extreme angles, unexpected perspectives, and tilted horizons in his photographs. He was highly influential among photographers and a leader of the innovative artists' group Oktober. He made many efforts to comply with official policy, but he was increasingly condemned by authorities. For his 1933 assignment to document the building of the White Sea Canal he restrained—slightly at least—his normal use of extreme angles in favor of making a straightforward record. Rodchenko was a brilliant graphic designer in addition to being a talented innovator in photography. He designed the White Sea Canal issue of *USSR In Construction* together with his wife Stepanova. But official condemnation led him to become less resolute in his artistic convictions after the mid-1930s. He died in 1956.

IVAN SHAGIN was born into a peasant family in the Yaroslav district in 1904. His father died when he was eleven, and shortly afterward his mother sent him to Moscow to work in a small shop. He left the

capital to be a sailor on a Volga steamer, then returned in 1924, finding work in various Moscow enterprises as a laborer and a salesman. He had taken up photography as a hobby in 1919, and in 1930 he began working as a press photographer for the newspapers *Nasha Zhizn and Kooperativnaya Zhian* and for the state agricultural publishing house Selchozgiz. He enjoyed his photographic subjects and had the talent to express his pleasure in the end result. In 1933 he got a job with the youth newspaper *Komsomolskaya Pravda* and stayed there until 1950. He tackled themes from industry to agriculture to sports to the Red Army and the Soviet navy and air force. Eventually his work appeared in *USSR In Construction* and in illustrated books. From 1950 on Shagin worked for *Pravda,* Novosti, and several book publishers. He died in 1982.

ARKADY SHAIKHET was born in the town of Nikolayev in 1898. After finishing primary school he became a locksmith's apprentice. He moved to Moscow in 1918 and four years later got a job as a retoucher for a portrait photographer. He left the portrait studio to become a photojournalist for the popular publication *Robochaya Gazeta*. In 1924 he began to work for *Ogonyok*. During the 1930s he produced photographs for *USSR In Construction* and, under the direction of Lazar Mezhericher, contributed pictures to the project "Twenty-Four Hours in the Life of the Filippov Family." During the 1940s, Shaikhet, like many of his colleagues, photographed the war. He died in 1959.

ARKADY SHISHKIN, the son of a carpenter, was born in 1899 in the village of Kukara in the Vyatka district (now Kirov). He served as an apprentice in a Kazan portrait studio then moved to Petrograd where he took a film projectionist course. After the Revolution he opened a photography studio in the town of Yekaterinenburg. From there, in 1918, he volunteered for the Red Army. When he was demobilized in 1922, he returned to Kukara and worked for a number of local newspapers and magazines, including Moscow's *Krestianskaya Gazeta*. He moved to Moscow in 1925. His primary photographic subject was daily peasant life, including collectivization. When World War II reached the Soviet Union he went to the front, first as a soldier then as a photographer. Afterward he continued to photograph as he had before and also experimented with color photography. He died in 1985.

LEONID SHOKIN was born in 1896 about a hundred miles north of Moscow in the town of Kimry on the Volga. For his fifteenth birthday his father gave him a camera, and he loved photography from then on. By 1918 he had shown skill and gained a reputation as a promising young talent. Between 1923 and 1928 he made romantic, soft-focus, pictorialist images in the artistic fashion of the times. His primary subjects were Kimry's traditional trades—producing shoes and farming the land. His photographs were exhibited both inside and outside the Soviet Union until 1930. In that year he was labeled a "formalist" and accused of poorly depicting workers who were building Socialism. As government control over photography tightened, the local Russian Photographic Society and photography magazine were shut down and it was impossible for Shokin to continue to pursue his pictorialist approach. During World War II the NKVD police entered his house and destroyed much of his archive while he was away fighting. Afterward he photographed and taught in the approved style. He died in 1962.

ANATOLY SKURIKHIN was born in the town of Kotelnich (formerly the Vyatka district, now the Kirov district) in 1900. He studied at the Higher Artistic-Technical Workshop in Vyatka and began to photograph while searching for nature subjects to paint. After his first scenic photographs were published in 1928, he moved to Moscow, studied at the State Art and Technical Workshops, and, in 1930, got a job at the newspaper *Komsomolskaya Pravda.* "My art school experience contributed to the quality of my photography," he once said. "The general culture of painting and my knowledge of the fundamentals of composition both helped." Skurikhin went on to work for *Izvestia,* documenting Stalin's first Five Year Plan, producing heroic images of factory workers and machines that exaggerated the scale of both. He photographed the Magnitogorsk and Kuznetsk steelworks and the Komsomol blast furnace and sunlit workshops, monumental depictions that were republished many times. He planned each shoot ahead of time down to the smallest detail, everything staged and posed. Skurikhin also photographed rural and agricultural subjects—tractors and harvests, farmers and their working wives. His early optimism and interest in the lyrical connection between man and nature remained intact through the years. In 1938 he photographed life in the collectives of the Lower Volga and Kirov districts and in the autonomous republics of Mari and Chuvash. He photographed for more than sixty years. He died in 1989.

SERGEI STRUNNIKOV was born in 1907 and attended the Moscow Film Technical secondary school, where he got interested in photojournalism. He began working for *Pravda* in 1932. During the thirties he photographed the icebreaker *Krasin* in the Arctic and construction in Central Asia and the Caucasus. He photographed Odessa, Moscow, and Leningrad during the war years and was killed near the town of Poltava in 1944 while on assignment.

VIKTOR TEMIN was born in 1908 in the Kazan Region on the Volga. By the time he was fourteen he was an accomplished photographer and obtained press credentials from a newspaper called *Izvestia Tat TSIK* (News of the Central Executive Committee of Tataria), later renamed *Krasnaya Tataria,* During the 1920s he photographed kolkhoz organization, cultural events, and famous people. In 1929, on assignment for *Krasnaya Tataria,* he photographed Maxim Gorky, who used the occasion to present him with a new Leica. Temin carried this camera for the rest of his life, using it in his increasingly successful work for *Pravda, Ogonyok, Izvestia,* and TASS. He covered the first Soviet expedition to the North Pole, the highly publicized Chelyskin rescue, other arctic expeditions aboard icebreakers, and a variety of airplane flights whose pilots (Chkalov, Baidukov, Belyakov, Osipenko, Grizodubova, Raskova) were made national heroes at the time. Temin covered four wars and the Nuremberg Trials and, like many of his colleagues, won numerous Soviet awards. He died in 1987.

GEORGY ZELMA was born in Tashkent in 1906. His father died several years before the Revolution of 1917, and in 1921 fifteen-year-old Georgy and his mother traveled for five weeks in a freight car of a train to reach Moscow. Zelma joined the photography club in his Moscow primary school and used an old Kodak box camera to take pictures in the city's suburbs and parks. He learned to shoot crowds by documenting scenes in the Proletkino film studios. His early pictures were published in the magazine *Theatr* and in other illustrated leisure and entertainment periodicals that were proliferating and providing opportunities for aspiring photographers in the 1920s. Zelma then went to work for Russfoto, shooting news stories, political demonstrations, and factory workers. After a several-month stint in a Petrograd portrait studio, he was assigned by Russfoto to his native city of Tashkent to cover Central Asia. There, between 1924 and 1927, his familiarity with the Uzbeki language an asset for access, he photographed the modernization and turmoil associated with women's liberation, mechanization, and education. *Sovetskoe Foto, Prozhektor, Pravda Vostoka, Kyzyl Uzbekistan,* and other publications printed his pictures as illustrations of the transformations brought about by Communism. Zelma left Tashkent when he was drafted into the army, returned to the city briefly after two years, then went to work for Soyuzfoto in Moscow, where he was introduced to the FED camera (the so-called Russian Leica). The new camera liberated him and expanded the range of his documentary work. He photographed Donbass factories, collective farms in the Tula region, and the Soviet air force, army, and navy. He contributed to *USSR In Construction,* collaborating with Max Alpert and Alexander Rodchenko on several special issues. In 1936 Zelma went to work for *Izvestia* and in 1937 photographed the construction of the Moscow-Volga Canal. During World War II he covered the southwestern front, Moldova, the Ukraine, Odessa, the Black Sea Fleet, and Stalingrad for *Izvestia.* Afterward he worked for the Novosti Press Agency and *Ogonyok* magazine. He died in 1984.

US

ESTHER BUBLEY was born in 1921 in Philips, Wisconsin. Her interest in photography inspired her to leave home after high school to study at the Minneapolis School of Design. Intrigued by the Farm Security Administration pictures she saw in newspapers and magazines, she moved to Washington at age twenty-two in hopes of photographing professionally. She worked first as a microfilmer in the National Archives, then as an FSA lab technician, always taking pictures after hours. Roy Stryker eventually gave her assignments covering the country's transition from the Great Depression to World War II, and from that Bubley went on to cover American life during the war itself. On one noteworthy Office of War Information assignment she recorded a round-trip Greyhound bus journey between Washington and Memphis in September 1943, just a month before Stryker left the OWI, which had subsumed the FSA in 1942, for his Standard Oil project. Bubley joined him at Standard Oil and continued her career as a freelancer, contributing to *Life* magazine and other publications. She died in 1998.

Marjory Collins, born in 1912, grew up in Scarsdale, New York, and studied photography informally with photographer Ralph Steiner during the 1930s. She was active in the Photo League, worked for the Associated Press, the Black Star Agency, and *US Camera* magazine, and then went to Washington to work for Roy Stryker. In November 1942 she photographed the wartime activities of Lititz, Pennsylvania—the residents' occupations and political, family, and community life. Her pleasant pictures captured the everyday gestures and accessories of individuals enjoying a stable, small-town existence. After World War II Collins took freelance government and commercial photography jobs in Alaska, Europe, and Africa. She stopped photographing in 1950, and died in 1985 in San Francisco.

Jack Delano was born in 1914 in Kiev and came to the United States with his family at age nine. He grew up in Philadelphia, studied at the Pennsylvania Academy of Fine Arts, and married graphic designer Irene Esser in 1940, the same year he was hired by Roy Stryker. His initial FSA assignments were short ones to nearby Maryland, Virginia, and North Carolina. His first major job for the agency, photographing migratory agricultural laborers, took him, along Route 1, from Florida to the Canadian border. He worked for Stryker for three years, much of it documenting the rural South, a region and way of life unfamiliar to him as an urban dweller. He also took assignments in Puerto Rico and the Caribbean. During World War II he produced photo essays on American industry and was drafted into the Air Corps. After the war Delano and his wife moved to Puerto Rico where they devoted themselves to socially motivated art projects. Delano died in August 1997.

Walker Evans was born in November 1903 in St. Louis, Missouri. He lived in Paris and tried his hand at writing before settling down in New York and taking up photography with a large-format camera. He was hired by the Resettlement Administration in June 1935, just before Roy Stryker got there, and was sent to West Virginia to photograph poverty and the alleviation of it by New Deal building projects. His relationship with Stryker was uneasy from the start, his demands and lack of obedience to Stryker's rules making life hard, but the work suited him perfectly. When Stryker faced budget problems in March 1937 he fired Evans, but the photographer's authority remained powerful. Together with Ben Shahn and Dorothea Lange, he had influenced other FSA photographers to produce documentary-style images devoid of theatrical composition and dramatic lighting. Evans's landmark, austere pictures rank high among the defining American images of the 1930s. In 1941 he and writer James Agee published their famous book, *Let Us Now Praise Famous Men,* featuring the lives of two Southern sharecropper families. From 1945 to 1965 Evans worked as associate editor at *Fortune* magazine where he produced, among other projects, a picture essay on the New York subways. He was charming, witty, difficult, and always had friends who helped him. He exhibited at the Museum of Modern Art, taught, and published books. He died in 1975.

Andreas Feininger, the son of painter Lyonel Feininger, was born in 1906 in Paris and spent his youth in Germany. He graduated summa cum laude from the Bauhaus in Weimar and then went on to study architecture in Weimar and Zerbst. He worked as an architect for several years while an interest in photography took root and grew. In 1939 he moved to New York City, abandoned architecture, and devoted himself entirely to photography. He worked as a freelance photojournalist with the Black Star photo agency, as a staffer at *Life,* and, between 1941 and 1942, as an FSA photographer for Roy Stryker. Over the course of his career, he applied the documentary approach he loved to nature and architecture studies as well as to street scenes. He exhibited, published, and taught widely.

Theodor Jung was born in 1906 in Vienna, Austria, arriving in Chicago as a six-year-old in 1912. Four years later he picked up his first camera and took pictures of the streets and buildings around him. In February 1934 he got work with the Federal Relief Administration in Washington preparing charts on unemployment. In his spare time he kept taking pictures. Learning about the FSA he thought it would offer a chance to see the country, improve his photography, and contribute to the welfare of people in need. Jung's assignments over his one-year stay with the agency took him to Maryland, Indiana, and Ohio. Back at headquarters in Washington he found himself at odds with Roy Stryker, who wanted his photographers to study their subject matter deeply before and while they worked. Jung believed his pictures would be stylistically and emotionally fresher if he didn't immerse himself in background information. A budget cut in May 1936 gave Stryker a reason to let him go. Jung continued his career in private business as an art director and photographer.

Dorothea Lange was born in Hoboken, New Jersey, in 1895 and studied photography in New York City after finishing high school. She moved to San Francisco in 1919 and spent the next decade earning her living there as a portrait photographer. In the early years of the Depression Lange got caught up in the increasing social and economic problems around her. She photographed San Francisco's unemployment, then documented the plight of migrant farm-workers in California's Imperial Valley and Nipomo, working closely with economics professor Paul Taylor whom she later married. Roy Stryker saw Lange's pictures of migrants in 1935 and offered her a job that August. She took the job but stayed away from Washington, keeping her Berkeley home as her base. She made pictures that would draw support for establishing migrant camps in California, and her photographs not only truly influenced public opinion, government policy, and other photographers, but illustrated the Depression with a unique humanity destined to define, more than any other single viewpoint, America's collective perception and memory of the era. Lange continued to photograph in the US and abroad throughout much of her life. Her pictures are still published and exhibited widely. She died in 1965.

RUSSELL LEE, born in 1903, didn't touch a camera until he was over thirty. Before then he studied chemical engineering and managed a roofing plant in Kansas City, Missouri. But bored with life as a manager, he went on a series of trips to explore his dream of becoming a painter. Along the way he discovered a calling in photography. In the winter and spring of 1935 and 1936 he roved the streets of New York with his camera, working on technique. He heard about the Farm Security Administration from Ben Shahn and joined its staff in September 1936, replacing Carl Mydans who had gone to *Life*. He stayed with the agency longer than anyone else, produced the most photographs, spent much of the year on the road, and enjoyed the itinerant life more than his colleagues did. Assignments took him to Oregon, the Ohio Valley, Minnesota, Wisconsin, and Michigan, where he investigated, in thorough detail, life in tightly knit communities. Unlike other FSA photographers, he took most pictures indoors—in homes, workplaces, churches, meeting halls—idealizing small-town life, recording how people managed to thrive in their customary environments in spite of the Depression. Lee stayed with the FSA until the formal end of the program in 1942. He was a war photographer during World War II and afterward taught at the University of Texas and the University of Missouri. He retired in 1974 and died in 1986.

CARL MYDANS studied journalism at Boston University, and after graduating in 1930 worked as a reporter in Boston and New York. Of the pictures he took during his lunch hours, a few were purchased by *Time* magazine, and this led to photographic assignments. An editor at *Time* recommended Mydans to Resettlement Administration officials who hired him and assigned him to photograph Washington, DC, Cincinnati, Maryland, and New Jersey. The pictures that resulted were eventually added to Stryker's file. Mydans moved to the Farm Security Administration in 1935 but stayed less than a year. Stryker sent him to cover cotton production, and he spent four months on the road, the first time he had been south and seen rural life. His second and final job for Stryker took him to New Hampshire and Vermont in October 1936. He refined his camera craft while at the FSA, becoming known for straightforward, unpretentious pictures. He then went on to join the first staff of *Life*. He covered World War II and afterward continued his work for the magazine, covering the Korean War and other events in the Far East and elsewhere. He died in 1997.

BEAUMONT NEWHALL was born in 1908 in Lynn, Massachusetts. He graduated from Harvard in 1935 and took a job as librarian at New York's Museum of Modern Art, remaining there for seven years. During that time he published *The History of Photography*, a pioneering book, now a classic. Always an advocate for photography as a fine art, Newhall served as founding curator of MOMA's photography department from 1940 until 1947. His active life in photography took him to Roy Stryker's office in Washington where he photographed the staff. He was curator of the International Museum of Photography at the George Eastman House in Rochester, New York, from 1948 to 1958, and director of that museum from 1958 to 1971. In 1971 he became an art professor at the University of New Mexico in

Albuquerque and moved to Santa Fe. Away from New York he remained active and respected in every segment of the photographic community. He died in 1993.

GORDON PARKS was born in 1912 in Kansas and grew up in Minnesota. During the Depression he worked as a musician, a dining car waiter on trains, and, finally, as a photographer in Minneapolis and Chicago covering fashion. He came to Washington and the FSA late, on a fellowship from a foundation devoted to studying the South and encouraging young black people professionally. Roy Stryker was not eager to have a black photographer on the FSA staff at first, fearing reactions inside and outside the agency, and Parks encountered bigotry in commercial establishments around the city as well. Angry about this and prepared to photograph the perpetrators of injustice, he credits Stryker with demonstrating to him the greater power of pictures showing the victims of bigotry. His most famous FSA pictures cover the personal life and work of Ella Watson, a government charwoman.

MARION POST WOLCOTT, born Marion Post in 1910 in Montclair, New Jersey, grew up in nearby Bloomfield, about twenty miles west of New York City. While she was studying in Vienna in 1933 a friend of her sister Helen introduced her to photography and, on her way back to the US in 1934, she purchased a Rolleiflex camera. She took a teaching job in New York and on days off began photographing, selling pictures to *Vogue, Life,* and *Fortune*. In 1937 she moved to Philadelphia to take a staff position at the *Philadelphia Evening Bulletin*, and in September 1938, at age twenty-eight, she was hired by Roy Stryker and began three intense, productive years of travel, mostly through the South, but in New England and the West as well. Feisty and committed, she remained with Stryker's program almost to the end. She resigned from the FSA in 1942, in fact retiring from photography altogether, to marry Lee Wolcott and raise a family. Though she occasionally photographed after her FSA years she never again fully devoted herself to photography. She died in 1990.

ARTHUR ROTHSTEIN was born in New York in 1915. In high school he took up photography as a hobby and built a basement darkroom in which he experimented with technique rather than aesthetics. Still consumed by photography at Columbia University, he founded the school's camera club, earned money by photographing for fellow students' dissertations, and was photography editor of the annual *Columbian*. Rothstein was a student of Stryker's and as a college senior in 1935 assisted him and another professor in assembling and copying photographs for a pictorial history of American agriculture that was never published. When Stryker went to Washington, Rothstein was the first photographer he hired. A key producer for the file, Rothstein spent five years with the agency, documenting, among other subjects, the lives of Virginia farmers evicted to make way for Shenandoah National Park, the Dust Bowl, cattle ranches in Montana, migrant workers in California, and the tenant farmer community of Gee's Bend, Alabama. He left the FSA in 1940 for a job at *Look* magazine.

BEN SHAHN was born in Lithuania in 1898 and arrived in New York with his family at age six. At thirteen he was apprenticed to a commercial lithographer. He supported himself with his new trade while honing his talents as a fine artist. His photography career began with pictures he took as references for his painting. Walker Evans, with whom he shared a Manhattan studio, instructed him in the use of a Leica, but the two took vastly different approaches to photography. Evans preferred the control of a large-format camera while Shahn liked the 35mm and used it casually, even attaching a right-angle viewfinder so he could point away from his subjects and give the impression he was photographing something else. In 1934 the Federal Emergency Relief Administration commissioned Shahn to produce a mural, and a year later he joined the Resettlement Administration as an artist. He contributed his views and photographs to Stryker's program as an unofficial, part-time advisor. Shahn's concerns with the big political and social issues of his day and his sensitivity to individual plights came through in his pictures.

ARTHUR SIEGEL was born in Detroit on August 2, 1913. He studied sociology at the University of Michigan and at Wayne State University, then, in 1937–38, went on to study photography under Laszlo Moholy-Nagy in Chicago. He worked prolifically for Roy Stryker in 1942–43 and finished the war serving as a photographer in the US Army Air Corps Aerial Photography Department. After the war he photographed for a variety of newspapers and magazines including the *New York Times* and *Life*. He spent the final decade of his life teaching photography in Detroit and Chicago. He died in 1978.

JOHN VACHON, born in 1914, came to Washington from his native Minnesota at age twenty-one to study at the Catholic University of America. In 1936 he took an entry level FSA job with the title Assistant Messenger. He had no intention of becoming a photographer until he began to respond to what he saw as he filed pictures. Encouraged by Walker Evans, Ben Shahn, Arthur Rothstein, and Stryker himself he practiced photographing around Washington on weekends. In October and November of 1938 Vachon went to Nebraska on his first extensive solo trip. He photographed the city of Omaha for Stryker and agricultural programs for the FSA's regional office. His pictures, anticipating America's postwar street photographers, showed a greater enchantment with everyday, urban scenes than with sociological issues. Vachon stayed on with Stryker at the Office of War Information and moved with him to Standard Oil. After the war he was hired by *Look* magazine and remained on staff there until his death in 1975.

ENDNOTES

1. Margarita Tupitsyn, *The Soviet Photograph 1924–1937* (New Haven: Yale University Press, 1996), 37.
2. B. Zherebtsov, "Arrangement of a Photo Series," *Proletarskoye Foto*, 9 (1932), 6.
3. Praskovya Angelina, *My Answer to an American Questionnaire* (Moscow: Foreign Languages Publishing House, 1951), n. p.
4. Studs Terkel, *Hard Times: An Oral History of the Great Depression* (New York: Pantheon Books, 1970), 20.
5. John Steinbeck, *The Grapes of Wrath and Other Writings 1936–1941* (New York: The Library of America, 1996), 458.
6. *This Fabulous Century 1930–1940* (New York: Time-Life Books, 1969), 30.
7. Hartley E. Howe, "You Have Seen Their Pictures," *Survey Graphic*, April 1940, n. p.
8. *The Ford Worker* IV, no. 1 (March 1996), 3.
9. Arthur Rothstein, *Arthur Rothstein: Words and Pictures* (New York: AMPHOTO, 1979), 6–7.
10. Ibid., 7.
11. Ibid., 8.
12. Ibid., 7–8.
13. Paul Hendrickson, *Looking for the Light: The Hidden Life and Art of Marion Post Wolcott* (New York: Alfred A. Knopf, 1992), 58.
14. Christopher Cox, *Dorothea Lange,* Masters of Photography Number 5 (New York: Aperture, 1981), 9.
15. Jack Delano, *Photographic Memories* (Washington, DC: Smithsonian Institution Press, 1997), 29.
16. Arthur Rothstein, *Arthur Rothstein: Words and Pictures* (New York: AMPHOTO, 1979), 7.
17. *Roy Stryker Papers 1912–1972* (microfilm reel 6, film no. 8521, The Library of Congress).
18. Ibid.
19. Arthur Rothstein, *Arthur Rothstein: Words and Pictures* (New York: AMPHOTO, 1979), 10.
20. *Roy Stryker Papers 1912–1972* (microfilm reel 6, film no. 8521, The Library of Congress).

21. Paul Hendrickson, *Looking for the Light: The Hidden Life and Art of Marion Post Wolcott* (New York: Alfred A. Knopf, 1992), 60.
22. Ibid., 136.
23. Ibid., 146.
24. Miles Orvell, "John Vachon: On the Road in Iowa," *Doubletake*, Winter 1997, 104.
25. Ibid., 106.
26. Lazar Mezhericher, "A Piece of Enormous Educational Power," *Soviet Foto* (1930), n. p.
27. Margarita Tupitsyn, *The Soviet Photograph 1924–1937* (New Haven: Yale University Press, 1996), 104.
28. Peter Galassi, "Rodchenko and Photography's Revolution," *Aleksandr Rodchenko,* essays by Magdalena Dabrowski, Leah Dickerman, Peter Galassi (New York: The Museum of Modern Art, 1998), 129.
29. Lazar Mezhericher, "Here and Over There: The Photo Post Card as a Bolshevik Information Medium," *Proletarskoye Foto,* 3 (1932), n. p.
30. Lazar Mezhericher, "Commercial Photography and Modern Western Photographic Art," *Soviet Foto,* 2 (1936), 16–18.
31. B. Zherebtsov, "Arrangement of a Photo Series," *Proletarskoye Foto,* 9 (1932), 10.
32. Max Alpert, "Socialism Recasts Man," *Proletarskoye Foto,* 7–8 (1932), n. p.
33. Vladimir Nikitin, "Struggle In Soviet Photography" (St. Petersburg: unpublished manuscript, 1995), n. p.
34. Ibid.
35. Ibid.
36. *Soviet Foto,* 2 (1940), 8.
37. Vladimir Nikitin, "Struggle In Soviet Photography" (St. Petersburg: unpublished manuscript, 1995), n. p.
38. *Roy Stryker Papers 1912–1972* (microfilm reel 6, film no. 8521, The Library of Congress).

ACKNOWLEDGMENTS

THE PHOTOGRAPHS IN THIS BOOK WERE SELECTED for their aesthetic and thematic content. No attempt was made to include pictures from every prominent government photographer of the decade or to sum up the life's work of any particular photographer. My aspiration was to convey the diversity of themes and the high aesthetic achievement of both groups of photographers and, through showing their best work, to pose important questions on these pages.

I planned to collect pictures from newly opened Soviet archives and recently accessible families and to examine them in relation to photographs filed in the Library of Congress. The sheer quantity of material, the logistics of borrowing the pictures, and the difficulty of finding the scattered photographs in Russian homes and neglected archives was more than I had anticipated. The following people in Russia began as generous contributors and grew to be partners in this enterprise: Nikolai I. Romanov (coordination, translation); Yuri A. Rybchinski—Museum of Photographic Collections (research and logistics); Felix Rosenthal (consultation); Yevgeny Y. Berrezner—ROSIZO (consultation); Alexander L. Lapin (printing, quality control, research); Olga F. Romanova (research).

Philip Brookman, Curator of Photography and Media Arts at the Corcoran Gallery of Art in Washington, DC, saw something in *Propaganda & Dreams* when I brought it to him in 1996. His endorsement, and through him the Corcoran's, gave the project life and allowed me to develop it and build it to completion.

Thurston F. Teele, President and CEO of Chemonics International, and Ashraf W. Rizk, executive vice president and CFO, also understood and believed in *Propaganda & Dreams* immediately. The resulting initial research grant from Chemonics gave me the resources to begin work in earnest.

Key professional support for *Propaganda & Dreams* came from Walton Rawls, editor, book coordinator, and all-around advisor. Professional support also came from Robert Zueblin, editor at Edition Stemmle in Zurich, and from Beverly Brannon and Verna Curtis, curators of prints and photographs at the Library of Congress. They all brought the priceless qualities of intelligence, experience, and enthusiasm to this project, and I'll forever appreciate my good fortune to have worked with them.

Medha Patel, Paul Roth, and Emily Hartmen provided indispensible help with research.

Alex Castro gave his immense talent to the book's design. The fine result, I feel, evokes the 1930s, features the timeless quality of the photographs, and remarkably adds up to a handsome modern book.

I also thank my colleagues and friends who in a daily way gave advice and support whenever I was in need, which was often, especially Sam Abell whose creativity and generosity seem boundless. And I thank Kevin Mulroy whose publishing insights proved indispensable, Mary Meade Nash (for Russian translation as well as generous friendship), Dena Andre and Ali Kahn for consistent belief in me and in this project.

Most of all, I am grateful to Avrom, Naftali, Oren, and Ronnit—they give meaning to everything undertaken.

CREDITS

The following lenders provided the photographs on the pages indicated:

Balashikha Lore and History Museum, 120; Kirov Museum of Local Lore, 99.

Sergei N. Burasovsky, 95, 107, 131; Yelena Chernevich, 69; Valery Ya. Cherniyevsky, 30, 126; Valentin A. Gorlov, New Gallery, 68; Alexei Loginov, 132.

Private Collector, Moscow, 1, 28, 87, 92, 94, 130, 133, 134, 135, 136.

Galerie Alex Lachmann, Cologne, Germany, 36 (both), 37 (top), 80, 85, 96, 101, 106, 118, 122, 123, 124 (both), 125, 127, 141; Paul and Teresa Harbaugh, Denver, Colorado, 65 (bottom), 84, 110, 129; Denver Art Museum, 114; Howard Schickler Fine Art, New York, 65 (top), 66, 82; Steven Kasher Gallery, New York, 10, 39, 89, 91.

Courtesy of the Fogg Art Museum, Harvard University Art Museums, Gift of Bernarda Bryson Shahn (Reproduction photograph by David Mathews), 9, 29.

Copyright the Dorothea Lange Collection, The Oakland Museum of California, City of Oakland. Gift of Paul S. Taylor, 42, 50 (top), 181, 183, 210.

Metropolitan Museum of Art, Ford Motor Company Collection, Gift of Ford Motor Company and John C. Waddell, 1987 (1987.1100.22), 210.

Howard Greenberg Fine Art, New York, 148 ©Estate of Arthur Rothstein, 159 © Estate of Jack Delano, 178.

National Archives, Records of the Civilian Conservation Corps, 71.

Quotation by Alexander Rodchenko, page 30, is from *Rodchenko Photography 1924–1954* by Alexander Lavrentiev. The poem titled "The Last Toast," page 26, is from *Poems of Akhmatova*, Selected, Translated, and Introduced by Stanley Kunitz with Max Hayward. ©1972, 1973 by Stanley Kunitz with Max Hayward. Quotations by Lincoln Kirstein, pages 9 and 29, are from Walker Evans, American Photographs ©1938 by Walker Evans and ©1988 by the Museum of Modern Art, New York. Reprinted by Permission.

In addition, these Russian critics, curators, photographers and their families generously gave time, insights, and photographs to *Propaganda & Dreams:*

Mark B. Markov-Grinberg, Yevgeny A. Khaldei , Anna E. Khaldei, Alexander N. Lavrentiev, Pavel V. Khoroshilov, Sergei N. Korolev, Dmitri D. Debabov, Timor Zelma, Klavdia N. Ignatovich, Agnia P. Khalip, Vera S. Petrusova, Vladislav V. Mikosha, Jemma S. Firsova, Nina Y. Lipskerova, Vladimir A. Nikitin, Grigory M. Chudakov, Valery T. Stigneyev, Maria A. Zhotikova, Valentina M. Shishkina, and Natalia D. Ukhtomskaya in memory of her mother Lilya Ukhtomskaya.

Yet more discoveries and insights on Soviet photographs came from:

The Central Moscow Archive of Documents on Special Media
The Russian State Archive of Cinema and Photo Documents (Krasnogorsk, Moscow Region)
The Russian State Archive of Literature and Art *(Our Achievements* Magazine Archive)
The Central State Archives of Cinema, Photo, and Phono Documents of St. Petersburg